make
your
own
rules
cookbook

ALSO BY TARA STILES

BOOKS

Make Your Own Rules Diet*

*Slim Calm Sexy Yoga:
210 Proven Yoga Moves for Mind/Body Bliss*

*Yoga Cures: Simple Routines to Conquer
More Than 50 Ailments and Live Pain-Free*

DVDs

*Jane Fonda's Workout:
Daily Yoga with Tara Stiles*

Tia Mowry's Calm & Core Yoga Series with Tara Stiles

This Is Yoga

Yoga Transformation Series (with Deepak Chopra)

*Available from Hay House

PLEASE VISIT:

Hay House USA: www.hayhouse.com®
Hay House Australia: www.hayhouse.com.au
Hay House UK: www.hayhouse.co.uk
Hay House South Africa: www.hayhouse.co.za
Hay House India: www.hayhouse.co.in

TARA STILES

make your own rules cookbook

More Than 100 Simple,
Healthy Recipes Inspired
by Family and Friends
Around the World

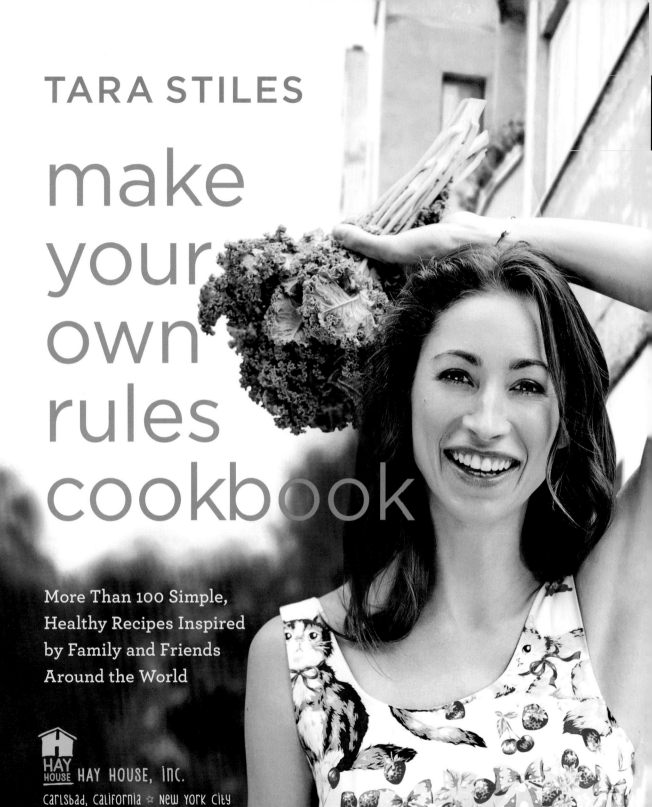

HAY HOUSE, INC.

Carlsbad, California ✫ New York City
London ✫ Sydney ✫ Johannesburg
Vancouver ✫ Hong Kong ✫ New Delhi

Published and distributed in the United States by: Hay House, Inc.: www.hayhouse.com
Published and distributed in Australia by: Hay House Australia Pty. Ltd.: www.hayhouse.com.au
Published and distributed in the United Kingdom by: Hay House UK, Ltd.: www.hayhouse.co.uk
Published and distributed in the Republic of South Africa by: Hay House SA (Pty), Ltd.: www.hayhouse.co.za
Distributed in Canada by: Raincoast Books: www.raincoast.com
Published in India by: Hay House Publishers India: www.hayhouse.co.in

BOOK DESIGN
Charles McStravick

PHOTO CREDITS
Photos on pages iv, title page, x, xvi, xix, xx, 2, 16, 40, and 224 by Winnie Au, www.winniewow.com

Photos on pages 38, 44, 48, 52, 58, 64, 68, 74, 80, 82, 84, 86, 88, 94, 100,
104, 110, 118, 120, 124, 132, 134, 138, 144, 148, 150, 152, 156, 158, 162, 166, 172,
176, 188, 192, 194, 198, 203, 207, 210, and 214 by Andrew Scrivani

Images on pages 15, 19, 36, 46, 47, 56, 92, 98, 108, 114, 130, 136, 140, 142,
146, 170, 186, 190, 204, 213, 222, and 228 under license from Shutterstock.com

Image on page 60 courtesy of Thinkstock

All other photos courtesy of Tara Stiles

Cataloging-in-Publication Data is on file at the Library of Congress

Hardcover ISBN: 978-1-4019-4436-0

10 9 8 7 6 5 4 3 2 1
1st edition, November 2015

PRINTED IN
THE UNITED STATES OF AMERICA

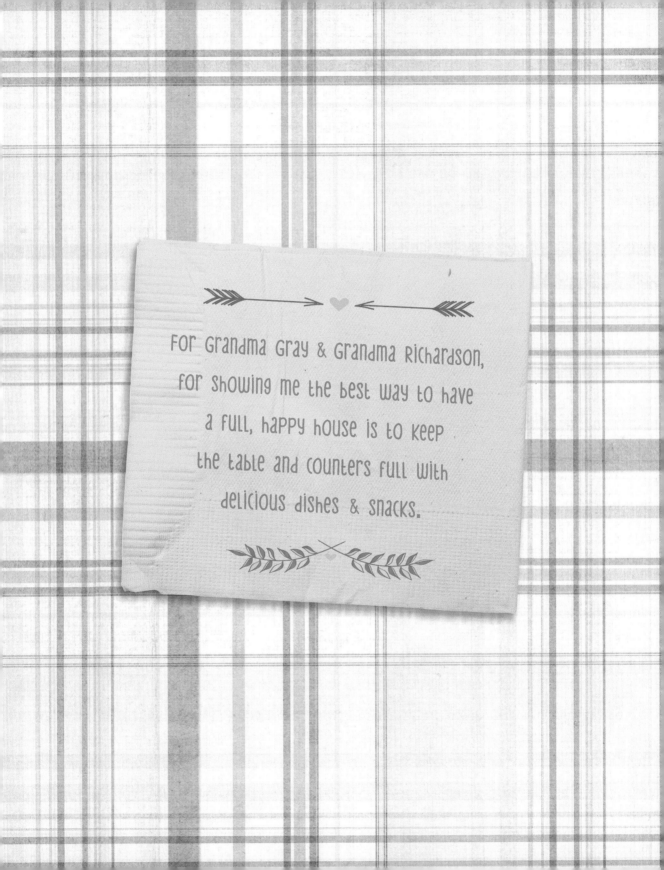

For Grandma Gray & Grandma Richardson,
for showing me the best way to have
a full, happy house is to keep
the table and counters full with
delicious dishes & snacks.

contents

foreword
by kris carr

Hiya, Gorgeous!

I'm so thrilled you are here. You're about to embark on a fabulous adventure in health and happiness—through cooking! *Make Your Own Rules Cookbook* is your passport to delightful dishes sure to appeal to everyone in your tribe.

My friend Tara travels the globe spreading her sunshine and sparkling yoga vibes to everyone she meets. I'm so psyched about her latest mission: to lure you back into the kitchen with simple and delicious meals that will inspire you to follow your intuition, explore your creativity, and nourish your beautiful body.

A major aspect of our health and well-being is our community, the people we keep around us. Sharing meals and exchanging recipes with those we love most is an age-old tradition that keeps us happy and healthy, and celebrates the unique gifts we all have to offer. With this in mind, *Make Your Own Rules Cookbook* is filled with more than 100 plant-based recipes from friends, family members, chefs, yoga teachers, and other kickass wellness warriors from all around the globe. Blending her hearty Midwest-inspired dishes with more exotic fare, from Malaysia, India, Japan, Russia, Thailand, Cuba, and more—Tara brings the world to you!

In *Make Your Own Rules Cookbook,* Tara shows that making healthy, delicious food can be easy and fun. From her tantalizing spin on classic green juices and smoothies, veggie burgers, kale salad, and miso soup, to her decadent and oh-so-simple Pad Thai, almond butter banana pancakes, and strawberry shortcake, she'll keep you satisfied and thriving from the inside

out. Tara takes you by the hand into an exciting realm of international and down-home cuisine, and encourages you to make it your own, improvise, and experiment. Make your own rules, *in the kitchen!*

I'm so proud of Tara's journey from model, to yoga teacher, to bona fide wellness leader, motivating millions to come together in sharing a big passion for feeling radiant inside and out, and not just living, but *thriving*. All of us have experienced, to some degree, periods where we were not feeling well, because of what we were eating or how we were treating ourselves. But the more of us that are dedicated to whipping up some crazy healthy meals for ourselves and those we love, the more awesomeness will be in us and all around us! How amazing is that?

Are you ready? As Tara reminds us, "If you can eat, you can cook!" so roll up your sleeves, pull up a chair, and prepare to enjoy every last bite!

KRIS CARR,

New York Times best-selling author of *Crazy Sexy Kitchen*

introduction

You know that old saying, "If you can eat, you can cook"? I truly believe that. I also believe that if you can imagine, you can create. That's what making your own rules in the kitchen is about, and that's what this book is about. It's about you. It's about the food you eat. It's about what you choose to put in your body on any given day. It's about how easy it is to have a life in the kitchen that doesn't take over your life elsewhere. It's also about having fun. That's right: fun.

So the only question is, if you're not in your kitchen, what's keeping you out? I hear so many people say that they're too busy, confused, unskilled, or simply uninspired. Whatever your reason, I'm here to show you that you can choose to step into the kitchen at any moment. And that's a beautiful thing. Trust me; you don't have to have tons of time or chef-like precision—or those insane chopping skills—to make delicious food. The recipes in this book will prove that to you.

I'm also here to show you that when you make time for creativity in the kitchen, you'll feel better, look better, and have more peace and focus in your life. Basically, you'll become more efficient and awesome, and you'll magically open up room for yourself to feel at ease and be excited by everything you experience.

Once you step into cooking, your creative potential ignites. So while these recipes are delicious, and you can certainly cook them exactly as is, I hope they inspire you to step out and try things on your own. Honestly, the secret ingredient to making your own rules in the kitchen is following your intuition with fierce trust. Doing this helps you get to know yourself. You find out what you like and what you don't. And, in turn, you create your own meals that make you feel fantastic from the inside out. When you are in the zone, the magic emerges and pours out of you—and not just in the kitchen.

Make Your Own Rules Cookbook is your guide to exploring the grand feast of life. It's filled with exciting delights, warm comforts, and exotic nourishment that will thrill all your senses and inspire your deepest desire to enjoy the wonderful experience of being you. In these pages you'll find some of my favorite recipes: some that were inspired by my childhood on a farm in Illinois, and some that come from my travels around the world. All of them are delicious. All of them are simple. And all of them are healthy. I hope they help you feel amazing.

Welcome to the massively bountiful buffet! Soon you'll be creating your own magnificent meals filled with heaps of love and loads of special sauce. And not long after, you'll start to experience the joy and excitement of life that is inspired by being truly nourished. So let's swap some recipes, discover new ingredients, blend unexpected cultures, and spend endless hours in creative exploration. It's time to eat!

PART
ONE

getting ready

my food rules

If you're familiar with me or with Strala Yoga, you won't be surprised to hear my singular rule for eating: eat what makes you feel great. Sadly, this is something that many of us don't do. Too often we get trapped in rules and restrictions. Food becomes the enemy. We label it strictly good or bad. We judge ourselves for how we eat. This is when the experience of eating can feel awful, like a trap we set for ourselves. Calories in and calories out can be a transactional nightmare. Our relationship to what we eat, how much we eat, and how we feel about the whole process is stressful, tense, and full of fear. When we don't know better, we think that living in restriction is the best way.

Thankfully there is an alternative to this funky fear programming: feeling great and looking great can exist in harmony. Our experience of eating can be joyful, loving, exciting, and nourishing. And the amazing thing that happens when we make this shift is that our fears subside and our bodies actually get stronger and more radiant. Our minds become sharp, clear, and expansive. And our lives get really fun and free.

When we realize that embodying radiance is actually easy and pleasurable, participating in the process of self-care becomes an awesome daily experience. And this includes eating. Once you get in tune with what makes you feel good, you'll crave it. While we all sometimes need (yes, *need*) a cookie, for the most part, our bodies want healthier options. It may sound wacky, but you'll actually stop reaching for the things that aren't great for you, like fried, junk, and processed foods, and you'll get legitimately psyched about veggies, fruits, grains, spices, and foods that give you more energy and life. Practicing restriction becomes silly and obsolete when you become interested in cooking because you get sensitized to what makes you feel amazing. If you are willing to explore and drop the rules, you are open to a limitless universe of options.

This "have what you want" food philosophy isn't something I've made up or only experienced for myself. After living this way for a while, people started to see a difference in me. They asked the usual question, what diet are you on? I'd tell them about my kitchen explorations and how these opened my eyes to what really made me healthy. I'd go on about simply eating what I wanted—what made me feel good—and they'd look at me a little funny. But that didn't stop me. Soon I was sharing simple recipes with my friends, gently suggesting that they add their own favorite flavors. My friends not only began following my recipes, but also started improving them so they would work better in their own lives. Weeks later, I'd see my pals, and they would feel great and have loads of energy.

This is what I want for you, too. Explore. Eat. Pay attention to your body. And, most of all, don't feel guilty; just learn and change accordingly. You can break the binge-and-purge, punishment-and-reward, diet-and-fail cycle. You can have what you want, but you have to get your explorer's hat on.

FROM DELIVERY TO DIY

When I first moved to New York City, I was like a lot of young people getting their start in the world: always on the go. Whether I was running to a gig, meeting up with friends, or exploring the city, hunger, as it does, set in several times a day, and the easiest thing to do was to pick something up on the go or order delivery. Food became an order away and a last-minute problem to be solved instead of an enjoyable process of creating and celebrating.

From a cultural and diversity perspective, I was in heaven in my early days in the city. A local falafel stand became the provider of my regular comfort meal. Crepe and ice cream shops served up my desserts. I would discover India in New York City through quirky food trucks and stands. And, of course, the quest for the best slice of New York pizza had to occur several times a week. I was eating pretty cheap and having a lot of fun. I rarely spent more than $6 on a meal—an impressive feat—but I wasn't exactly getting a lot of nutrition.

Back in those days, taking time to cook was the furthest thing from my mind. It seemed like a waste of time. I didn't see the value in investing in groceries, let alone kitchen gear, when I could just head outside and find something easy, delicious, and cheap. It just didn't make sense.

My energy levels, naturally, adjusted according to my eating habits. A hungry-full, spike-crash cycle set in. I wasn't paying attention to the quality of what I was eating; I was simply eating to satisfy hunger. This meant that I didn't think much about the effects of what I was consuming. I was young and healthy, and I felt invincible. But the reality was that my mood was all over the place. My body felt okay but not great, no matter what kinds of exercise I did. While I didn't consciously make the connection at that point, this was all related to what and how I was consuming. If I wanted energy, I would down some caffeine or grab some sugar. If I had a tough day, I'd grab some fries and pig out. Obviously, these food choices didn't exactly heal my mood, but I wasn't quite ready to invest in discovering a better way.

Subconsciously, however, I was already on a different path. I had explored the teachings of Eastern and classical arts for a long while. And soon enough I started feeling a desire to change. Each day a voice shouted louder in my own mind: *Take care of yourself!* That statement kept ringing through my brain, and I felt a little strange about it, to be honest. It was like my mom telling me to get plenty of sleep and take care, but this time it was coming from inside me. Mom wisdom must come from a deeper, more internal source of power. It turns out that it's not just nagging; it's true. So I began to internalize all that I had studied along with my desire to change. I put everything in a big pot, stirred it, and let it simmer. I knew I was cooking up something, I just didn't know quite how spicy it would turn out.

SPACE CRAVING

What eventually pushed me over the edge into a healthier life was a desire for space. I think this is a familiar feeling for a lot of us when we are looking for a positive change in our lives. Sure, we want to eat better, feel better, and have more fun and satisfaction in our lives, but ultimately the desire is for space. We start to feel pinned down by whatever is lousy in our lives. So we need to create space that will allow us to make changes. We need a new world: an open place where we can paint the sky, explore the forest, and swim in the ocean in whatever way feels right. We need to create this new world in order to create the new us. Every little bit you create leads to the potential for more space. And if you keep building on this, you create an open and expansive life where you are free to be your best self.

When I started wanting more and more space, I realized that I was ready for a life transition. Even though I was technically grown up, I was ready to grow into myself. I was starting to get excited about the possibility of having more energy in my life, so I needed to prepare.

I started to prioritize creating more physical and emotional space. I carved out time to slow down, relax, focus, and reflect. Some days, this turned into a 20-minute journal-writing session. Other days, it took the shape of a 15-minute home meditation and yoga practice, or I simply allowed myself a few moments to rest, lie down, and do nothing. By not filling every moment of my time with busy-work, I started to create more space to propel my life into a better place. It helped break my cycle of being tired, stressed, and worn out. These little bits of me-time allowed my creativity to open and my energy levels to rise, and I had a whole new feeling of room in my life. Then I suddenly had the urge to cook.

I wanted to explore, try, and fail (or succeed!) with creating food sensations. I no longer wanted to order from a menu. So, armed with a dazzling desire and a bit of spunk, I headed out to get my tools. Grocery store, here I come!

My first several trips to the market were pretty laughable and slightly embarrassing. I had no idea what to put in my cart. My shopping experiences had been pretty limited up to this point. Hummus and crackers and those bags of baby carrots are healthy, right? Those, along with cereal, bread, and peanut butter, were my staples, thus putting my cooking abilities right up there with the average 8-year-old. I was qualified to pour a bowl of cereal and fix myself a snack. That was pretty much it.

But it was now or never. I dove right in, heading to the scariest section of the store first: the edges, where all the fresh veggies were staring me down, mocking my abilities. Giant stalks of kale, loose mushrooms, and exotic spices that I had only read about in the food glossies went into my cart. I became enchanted with the Asian section. All those noodles, spices, and pastes perplexed me in the best way. I got a few of each and decided I would figure it out as I went along. I had no plan for dishes. I just gathered a bunch of high-quality ingredients and went crazy experimenting. I felt that nothing could go too wrong. In a worst-case scenario, I would make a bunch of meals that didn't taste great but were really healthy.

At home I experimented with soups, boiling down veggies and spices. Most of my big mistakes produced soups that were either a strange color or way too spicy.

I still ate all my mistakes out of principle. These were good ingredients and I was lucky to have them. Soon salads and sandwiches became fun, easy, and quick. I even got a little fancy toasting the bread and cutting it diagonally. It was the little things that made me feel gourmet.

I loved experimenting with dressings, blending up fresh ginger, lemon, and spices. Not willing to sacrifice indulgence, I started to seek out loads of rich, savory ingredients. I got into different kinds of mustards, coconut milks, almond butters, and healthy oils—really anything that was creamy. I mixed pretty much everything together and shortly discovered not only my favorite ingredients but also crowd favorites from friends and family who were quickly becoming my brave taste-testers.

Through this stage of experimentation and play, I started to realize the importance of the process, not the goal. And I began to see my life as one connected whole. This was a new way of looking at life, and it was a big shift for me. I had been living my life in categories—work, play, good, bad, yes, no—and it was making me tense.

I think a lot of us do this. We look at life as a daily grind; we live for escape. Whether the escape is drinks after work, a wild weekend, or an epic vacation, we start to separate fun and no-fun, and a habit of punishment and reward gets ingrained. We eat well during the week, stay on track, go to work, and essentially have no fun. When it comes to the weekend, we let loose, all sorts of craziness happens, and we go out of control. I was living for the escape. Most of us have been there in one form of another.

So I started to shift out of necessity. I was tired of feeling tense, and my escape techniques of letting it all go with drinking, eating junk, and lazing about didn't work anymore. Getting interested in myself again and in spending time in the kitchen kick-started the transition from escaping to enjoying my life. It gave me the energy and passion to create an existence that fueled me and kept me inspired all the time.

 WE ARE ONE

One of the things that has become crystal clear to me in my kitchen explorations is that I love variety, both in my cooking and in my day-to-day activities. In the life I've carved out for myself, variety takes center stage. My work takes me to a lot of different countries and puts me in front of a lot of uniquely amazing people. Even when I am at Strala in New York City for a while, it's incredible to meet and hear the stories of the passionate and interesting people who come through the doors. I thrive in the energy of the diversity and culture, and the backgrounds and experiences of these individuals. And the deeper understanding I've come to through these experiences is that we're all the same: we all have the desire to feel great, explore, and share. We are linked by a longing to feel full in our hearts, radiant in our bodies, expansive in our minds, and connected in our souls.

This idea has grounded and sustained my energy, health, and attitude while I have bounced around the globe. It helps me feel at home wherever I am. With this attitude, I am uplifted and inspired by each moment, in each place, by each person, and with every connection.

I think this desire to connect is innate in most of us. We're here to expand, grow, and help. We're here to laugh, cry, and be in awe. We're here to enjoy, delight, relax, inspire, and become whole. And at a larger level, we are propelled to do better in our world by our links to one another.

We each have unique gifts, and when we're nourished and celebrated, our individuality has massive potential. And when we see the individuality of those around us as a precious gift, we are in the right state of expansive mindfulness to live out something incredible.

Anything that inspires self-exploration will guide you toward your own unique gift and bring a balance to your life that will help you see the unique gifts in others. That's why I say to go crazy in the kitchen. Delve into the process. Learn what sets you aflame. Learn what angers you. Learn how to connect with your true spirit.

DIPPING BACK TO GO FORWARD

One of the best ways to figure out what you want—both in and out of the kitchen—is to look back and see where you've been, what has made an impression on you, what you'd like to let go, and what you'd like more of in your life. Reflection is a great tool for growth. Think of it as research for the most delicious recipe you're going to make: you. Just don't get stuck too far in the past and miss out on everything that's happening right now.

As I look into my own past, I see carefree childhood memories of being much more interested in the final product of cooking than in the process. When it was time for supper, a nourishing spread would show up in front of me. I was constantly on the go, very interested in being outside, climbing trees, dancing, and discovering the world. Food was fuel that appeared on the table conveniently delivered by Mom, Grandma, aunts, and sometimes Dad when Mom was unavailable. Dinner by Dad was generally burned toast, eggs, and breakfast things that emerged out of a sea of smoke, with a detector beeping in the background. On these rare occasions of Dinners by Dad, my brother and I were mostly excited to use the ketchup. We survived just fine. We appreciated the effort and the nourishment.

On days when my hunger overtook me—usually when the sun went down after a long day of playing outside, or when I came home from a long night of dance practice—I found the need to physically place myself in the kitchen closer to the food while it was cooking to assure myself that supper was coming soon. I would receive the occasional task of snapping peas or washing the dirt off vegetables that had come fresh from the garden. But all the preparing, seasoning, stirring, and timing that my mom was orchestrating was, more or less, a mystery to me. I waited very impatiently until our yummy spread was ready. The kitchen always smelled like it was time to eat, no matter if it was or not. I always thought this endless torture was some sort of Appreciate Mom test. It worked. I would have starved without you, Mom. Thanks for feeding me with food and love for all those years.

As I was in my own kitchen, creating my own yummy spreads, I began to realize that my entire life had been focused on connection to self and protecting uniqueness.

In my youth, this took many forms, most of which were not in the kitchen. I would get incensed when I saw injustice that prevented people from being who they truly were. Whether it was bullying, unfairness shown by an authority figure, or people who weren't in a position to help themselves, I had a strong reaction. I'd interject and usually do something dramatic, though it wasn't always the best choice of action, like shoving a bully, protesting a teacher, or demanding that everyone give their lunch money to starving children in Africa. My strong demands were rarely welcomed. But I wanted everyone to be free from whatever was holding them back.

This attitude always led my career choices: I wanted to be a nun when I was 4 so I could help people; I also liked the idea of living cost-free. Then at 6, I made a hard turn when I learned that having resources put you in a good position to help others. So I switched my sights to becoming a stockbroker. Clearly, I gave that up.

When I moved to New York City, I made my living through dance, which I had spent my childhood studying and performing. I loved dancing and making people smile. My only issue with this career path was that I wanted the people in the audience to dance, too. Dance helped me find myself, and while many people told me that watching my performances helped them connect with their emotions, I couldn't believe that watching would have the same impact as doing. I wanted to perform *with*, not *for*, everyone. I also craved connection. Dance was fun and rewarding, but it wasn't making me feel as alive as I wanted.

And so I created Strala yoga, a natural mash-up of all my interests. Its aim is to help people connect and feel great from the inside out. The movements are designed to build strength, empower, and heal while being fun and uplifting. The last bit definitely steps away from the rules of traditional yoga, but stays right in line with how I live. Growing up, I always knew that things could change; what *is* doesn't have to *be*. This principle is what has guided me in the creation of this nontraditional form of yoga.

I take the same view on food and eating: what is doesn't have to be. The rules and restrictions placed on our eating don't have to be there. This philosophy is in full force in my kitchen. I break some of the normal rules of spice combination, textures, flavors, and so on. And I don't classify foods as good or bad. They are good *for me* or bad *for me* based on how they make *me* feel. I truly make my own rules. And by doing this, I help myself get sensitized to food, which is essential for connecting to what your body and mind really need to be at their best.

Lifting others from the injustices placed on them was the root of the battles I fought in my youth. Now my goal is to help you lift the injustices you place on yourself around food and eating. What you eat, how you eat, and how you feel about it all make up a huge part of your relationship with yourself, with others, and with the world.

We express ourselves through unique customs, prayers, rituals—and spices. Sometimes, we get it right and experience the beauty of balance; other times, we fall away from ourselves. The work we all do is about moving toward harmony and balance within ourselves. Once we find this balance, we can encourage others who have lost their way. We can help them find their way back.

Moving back to go forward is the way of nature. The waves retreat and roll in. The sun sets and rises. The flowers close and open. The process is fluid, circular, and big. The process creates and takes up space. Our lives are oceanic, and we can flow in the direction of our wildest dreams when we allow intuition and inspiration to be our fuel. Anything that helps us come back to our natural selves, whether it is exploring in the kitchen or connecting with people around us, helps us become more of who we truly are. Have fun discovering the infinite ways to express yourself, and you will learn to nourish not only your body, but also your mind, spirit, and soul. And then you will open yourself up to growth and joy in every area of your life.

Creating Space Meditation

Before you go into the kitchen, let's get down and dirty with a little exploration of your past—dip back to go forward. Sit however you feel comfortable. Close your eyes and allow your attention to drift inward. Watch your inhales and your exhales as they come and go. If you notice your mind wandering, see if you can guide your attention back. Take a gentle mental scan of your body from the top of your head down through your neck, your shoulders, your chest, your belly, your hips, your legs, and your feet. Move your body any way you like to get comfortable.

Take an easy mental journey into your past. Dive softly into your early years. Allow memories of meals, treats, and snacks to enter your mind. What was your favorite meal as a kid? Remember enjoying that meal. What about it made it your favorite? Did you have a hand in preparing it? Was there a specific place you enjoyed the meal? How did you feel when you enjoyed this meal?

Allow that feeling to dance through your body. Allow that feeling to warm you and bring a smile to your face. Allow that feeling to simmer through you. Now take a big inhale through your nose. Soak up the feeling. Hold all the air in for a moment. Allow your body to fill and be full. Allow the air to dance through your body while you hold it in. Open your mouth and exhale. Return to an easy pace of breath for a few moments. When you are ready, gently open your eyes. I hope you feel spacious, open, and ready to create.

ENERGY IS EVERYTHING

In addition to what you eat, how you feel when you eat matters. How you feel when you cook matters. How you feel about yourself all the time matters. How you feel is your energy, and your energy is what sends you crashing into the fade zone or skyrockets you into radical vibrancy. This book is my love letter to your energy.

Your energy has the potential to be incredibly expansive, ridiculously happy, and crazy awesome. I want that for you. I want that for me. When you have good energy, you feel great and you do great things. When you are in a good space with your energy, everything you do, think, and feel impacts the world for the better. Simple things like making friendly conversation with a stranger on the train or smiling at the people in line at the coffee shop may seem like small acts, but they can have a big impact that ripples out into the world. Good energy also allows you to do big things. You feel awesome, so you make great life decisions. You follow your intuition when it comes to picking career changes, family planning, self-care, and so much more. You can literally shift the experience you have by shifting your energy.

The simple act of getting in the habit of preparing our meals with mindfulness and playfulness helps us shift into a magical frame of body and mind. When we spend more time in the kitchen, we create the space for awesome vibes for our lives and the food we cobble together.

The contents of what we eat matter a lot, but we can't ignore how we feel and the energy we drizzle on our meals. By simply spending time getting our hands dirty in the kitchen, our creativity opens up, inspiration pours out, great energy sets the stage, and we consume healing and expansive awesomeness. Cooking transforms from a dreaded mandatory act to stay fueled to an exciting adventure in creativity and fun.

I'm excited for the shift when we collectively understand that it's not simply what we eat that shapes our health. How we feel during our meals is just as crucial as the nutrients on our plates. Of course, it's important to consume high-quality foods, as what we eat and drink on a daily basis factors big-time in our overall well-being. But it's a mistake to ignore our emotional life as a key ingredient in the process. Follow how you feel, and you will discover a rich layer of well-being that exists much deeper than the nutrients in your veggies. So are you ready to get your hands dirty and your belly happy?

get your kitchen groove on

I have a kitchen confession to make: even though I'm "into cooking" now and I know how great it is, it sometimes gets pushed aside for other tasks. When I get busy (and we're all always busy), cooking is the first thing to go out the window. Whether it's impossible to cook because I'm traveling so much, or I'm back from traveling and don't make the time—or I'm simply not in the mood to restock the kitchen—my direct link to fantastic energy gets zapped. During these busy spurts,

I find myself taking to the streets, hungry and without a plan, just like when I first arrived in New York City. Burritos, pizza, and take-out soups and salads happen more often than they should at my house. I get stuck when I'm unprepared. When I'm left with a cabinet presenting a lone half-empty bag of rice and a few spices, I'm not really able to stretch my imagination.

Owning up to my tendencies to let my kitchen time dwindle helps me bring mindfulness to self-care. It reminds me of how important it is to stay on top of loving myself. The more we practice taking care of ourselves, the more we can reverse whatever has taken us out of balance. When we take care of ourselves, we sway our way right back to that amazing, centered place. And this is much easier for me when I can jump right into the kitchen and start creating.

The truth is that I love spending time in the kitchen. Exploring, creating, tasting, and sharing food with friends and family is an act I receive great joy from. I aim to nurture this aspect of my life and discover endless dishes filled with delicious happiness for a long time. But to do this, I have to make sure I make the space and get into habits that make this easy. While grabbing a slice may be simple, you just don't get the same energy and joy from it that you do from a lovingly home-cooked meal. So let's clear some space to get our kitchen groove on.

PRE-PREP

Before we get cooking, and even before we go shopping, we have to do some cleansing. Don't worry; I'm not suggesting days upon days of lemon-water fasts until you drop. We're headed more along the lines of making mental space for ourselves and physical space in our kitchens for greatness. A calm mind and clear vision will help us create the kitchen setup that best suits us, taking into account both our desires and actual circumstances. Sometimes people feel like they can't start cooking because they don't have all the right equipment and they can't afford to buy it. Or because they have a mere 10 inches of counter space, so any prep work is going to be impossible. Whatever your thoughts are, you needn't worry. Anyone can do this, even with dull knives and a tiny workspace. Yes, it's true that there are *ideal* kitchens, but most of us have to deal with some less-than-ideal spaces. I'm here to tell you that it's totally doable.

Before you start clearing space in your actual kitchen, clear some space in your mind using the Creating Space Meditation on page 20.

Creating Space Meditation

Sit however you feel comfortable. Close your eyes and allow your attention to drift inward. Watch your inhales and your exhales as they come and go. If you notice your mind wandering, see if you can guide your attention back. Take a gentle mental scan of your body from the top of your head down through your neck, your shoulders, your chest, your belly, your hips, your legs, and your feet. Move your body any way you like to get comfortable.

Imagine your ideal kitchen. Imagine yourself in that kitchen with loads of open mental and physical space for exploration. What ingredients do you imagine in your fridge and cabinets? What's baking in the oven? Do you have an herb garden? What fruits and veggies are resting on the counter? What does the kitchen smell like? How do you feel in your ideal kitchen?

Allow that feeling to dance through your body. Allow that feeling to warm you and bring a smile to your face. Allow that feeling to simmer through you. Now take a big inhale through your nose. Soak up the feeling. Hold all the air in for a moment. Allow your body to fill and be full. Allow the air to dance through your body while you hold it in. Open your mouth and exhale. Return to an easy pace of breath for a few moments. When you are ready, gently open your eyes. I hope you feel spacious, open, and ready to create.

CLEANING UP YOUR SPACE

Now that you've cleared some space in your mind, it's time to turn to your kitchen. If you're anything like me, there are some things living in the back of your fridge that have been there for way too long. Heck, you may not even know what they are anymore! Or perhaps you have cabinets filled with who-knows-what from who-knows-when? All you know is that it's covered in dust and completely inedible. How is that stove looking? Mine gets pretty messy, especially when it hasn't been used in a while. What's in the oven? Baking sheets with old cookie crumbles? Yep, that's me. We're all guilty of letting things go, so let's band together and put a little time into cleaning.

The first step of any good cleaning is getting rid of what's bad. When you're looking through your kitchen, try to use an "everything must go" mind-set (unless it's fresh and you expect to use it). Are you hanging on to a super-old jar of pickles with a couple of lonely spears floating around? Do you have a half-eaten box of cereal from some time last year? Chuck it. I hear a lot of people say, "But that's wasteful." And my answer to them is, "No, it's not." If there is the possibility that the food is stale, and not just free of mold, toss it out. And then use this as a learning experience. Take note of the waste and vow not to buy these things again. It's a good practice—I promise. Better to toss it out than to hang on to what you'll never use. Trust me; you'll feel so much more satisfied when you're not piling new on top of old. Plus, you'll know what you really have and what you need to get.

Once your purge of old and bad things is complete, it's time to put in a little elbow grease and make your space shine. I know it's not fun, but again, it'll feel good. Scrub that stove. Pick the sticky stuff out of the fridge drawers. Wipe that old frosting off the backsplash (finally).

Gloves Out!

I've learned the sticky way that it's better to glove up than to get glommed on by mystery stale fridge goo. You're much more likely to actually get in there, toss out the old, and scrub out the gunk if you're properly protected.

Greening Your Home

Part of purging and cleaning your kitchen is going through the nonfood items you own to see if there's anything that could negatively impact your health. If toxins are hiding in your cleaning products, cookware, or any other household items, you should get them out of your home immediately. For a lot of things, I think you should keep what you have; don't waste your money on new things just to have new things. But there are certain things I'm not going to budge on, because I care about you and I want you to have a fair chance to radiate without getting sick.

For example, many companies that make cookware use perfluorooctanoic acid (PFOA), which is a key processing agent in making Teflon for nonstick and stain-resistant products. However, PFOA has been linked to cancer and birth defects in animals and thyroid disease in people. It is also in the blood of 95 percent of Americans. Thankfully, many companies have agreed to eliminate this harmful chemical by 2015, but only through a voluntary pact crafted by the Environmental Protection Agency. So throw out any nonstick products you have unless you know, without a doubt, that they don't contain PFOA. This is one thing I will insist on. I would come over and do it for you if I could cover the entire world of kitchens. That's how strongly I feel. Healthier alternatives are easy to come by, and they don't have to be expensive.

The same goes for the rest of the items listed in the table below, which I created based on information from the Environmental Working Group. Check out www.ewg.org to learn more about the impact of chemicals and toxins in your home and tips on greening up your living space.

make your own rules cookbook

TOSS THIS	WHAT IT CONTAINS	HARM IT CAN DO	USE THIS
Toxic cleaning products	Ammonia, sodium hydroxide, sodium hypochlorite	Trigger asthma attacks and cause respiratory damage and possibly cancer	Good old-fashioned soap and water, vinegar and water, or organic cleaning products without chemicals—check labels
Nonstick cookware	Contains perfluorinated compounds (PFCs)	Linked to ADHD and thyroid disease and is potent sperm killer, contributing to infertility	Glass, cast-iron, or stainless steel
Antibacterial soap	Contains triclosan	Disrupts thyroid function and hormone levels	Good old-fashioned soap and water
Roundup foods	Roundup herbicide	Affect defensive enzymes that we need to stay healthy, and reduce plants' ability to take up vital nutrients that we require for survival	Buy organic
Scented detergents	High levels of volatile organic compounds (VOCs)	Linked to asthma and cancer	Plant-based, unscented detergent
Plastic containers, cooking utensils, and canned foods	Bisphenol A (BPA)	Linked to male infertility, diabetes, and heart disease	Even plastics marked BPA-free leach measurable amounts of chemicals into your food; use glass, stainless steel, or bamboo, and paper instead of plastic plates for picnics; buy fresh or frozen fruits and veggies, and avoid cans and plastic containers as much as possible

So as you can see, this isn't about being trendy; it's about preventing serious problems like respiratory damage, thyroid disease, infertility, and cancer. Don't be scared, and do something today to green up your home.

SETTING UP YOUR SPACE

Once you get things cleaned and greened, it's time to move to a more fun part: setting up your kitchen. To do this, you'll want to look at all of the kitchenware you own. This will allow you to organize what you have and figure out what you'll need to buy. So lay everything out, and let's start looking at where things stand.

Must-Haves and Wish Lists

Being from rural Illinois, I was raised with the idea that the best way to live is to take good care of things and use them until they break—and then use them for something else. Famers are some of the oldest proponents of the "reduce, reuse, recycle" philosophy. Have you ever seen an old, broken-down tire posted on a fencepost as a No Trespassing sign? Perfect.

With these ideals in mind, I'm going to lay out my list of what you need for your kitchen. It's probably a bit different from what you'll find in other books, but it'll save you time, respect your budget, and take your cooking skills to the next level with ease.

You don't need to stock your kitchen with expensive equipment. For the most part, you can start with what you have; as long as you have the basics, you don't need the best version. Then, once you get going for a while, you'll have a clear idea of what you really need to upgrade or what you would like to upgrade. And at that point, you'll also know how wonderful this way of living can be, so spending money on more expensive items won't be as painful. It's easy to fall into the trap of buying the most expensive kitchen gear before you jump into cooking. But it's better to go through the process of investigating, clearing, and cleaning what we have so we can start where we are. Where you are is a great place to be. The time is always now, and you have everything you need to start creating.

Here are the basics of what you need to make all the food in this book:

KNIVES

Let's talk about knives, baby. Slicing and dicing to your heart's content is a big part of getting your culinary on. Having the proper tools to cut with is important, but even more important is your safety and the safety of those around you. Being the clumsy gal that I am, I waited for a long time until I explored the universe of grown-up kitchen knives. A sharp knife was one of my last kitchen hardware purchases, and the reason I had waited for so long was partly just a fear of slicing my fingers off. For this fine piece of equipment, if you're anything like me, you should wait to make the investment. Your usual kitchen knives will do just fine in chopping the produce and ingredients you'll be using most. And you don't need oodles of different sizes or types of knives. Make sure you have a couple of solid knives; nothing fancy is needed at the beginning. What you have laying around is probably good enough.

You'll know when you're ready to move into the world of ultrasharp knives. For me, strangely, it was an overpowering feeling. One day, I just *knew,* so I went out browsing and ended up with a private lesson from an in-store knife expert. He showed me how to slice carrots so thin that they looked like paper and melted in my mouth. It was like carrot butter. And then I was hooked. I left the store with a sharp knife, a sharpening stone, and a protective case. Honestly, my sharp knife doesn't get everyday use. I don't trust myself with it when I'm rushing to toss a salad together. But I do use it quite a bit on the weekends or at night when I'm preparing a relaxing dinner with friends.

CUTTING BOARD

Sharp knife or not, you're going to need a cutting board. Again, what you have will probably work. If you have to buy one, I suggest going with one that you like the look of and that is pretty sturdy. Avoid glass, though: it's a horror on knives and can break. Glass shards and sharp knives? Not a fun combo. So just pick up something small and simple that will do the trick. Make sure you get one that can be tucked away easily after use. The whole goal of a cutting board is to keep your counters free of slice marks. There are loads of adorable little cutting boards out there. In many ways, it's nice to have a tiny one because it's easy to clean and store.

A good cutting board can also be an investment piece that you can leave out on your kitchen counter. If you go with one that is beautiful in design, you won't want to hide it from view. For the longest time, I had a flimsy hand-me-down that I probably stole from the back of my mom's cabinet. It lasted for a while and did the job, but after getting serious about creating in the kitchen, I was craving a big hunk of something pretty for the counter. The big, beautiful buggers take some maintenance, but they look really sleek, too.

SKILLETS AND PANS

If you're going to invest in one or two new things in order to get inspired, I'd say go for this cookware. You're going to want at least one skillet and one saucepan, and having decent-quality ones can make a huge difference in whether or not you stick with cooking. Again, buying new ones isn't necessary, unless, of course, you have the unsafe nonstick versions that we talked about before. Opt for stainless steel, anodized aluminum (like All-Clad), cast-iron, copper, or ceramic. These are all safe options. One of my prized possessions is my giant cast-iron skillet. It's a big, heavy piece that sits proudly on my stove, making me feel safe, protected, and inspired to turn the heat on and whip up anything delicious.

BLENDER

There are all kinds of blenders out there in all sorts of price ranges. It can be crazy confusing. Luckily, this is an area where you have a lot of wiggle room. If you have an old blender lying around in the back of your cabinet or in a box in the closet, this is a great opportunity to give it a second chance. Most blenders will cream up all the basics that you'll be craving, like smoothies, dressings, and soups. The reality is that your old blender will simply test your patience more than the fancy high-speed models. With an inexpensive blender, you'll have to wait a bit longer for your spinach to get creamy in that smoothie, or for your soup to be pureed, but be encouraging of your little machine. It can do the work for you, and high-end blenders can cost in the realm of $700, so don't invest unless you've proven to yourself that you'll use it.

If you are ready for an upgrade, a high-speed blender will, admittedly, probably change your life. As an avid kitchen enthusiast, I use mine every day, often more than once. My staple morning smoothie is whipped up and creamy in moments. A soup that I want to blend up is pureed in an instant. As a bonus, I can do flashy tricks and make dishes that a back-of-cabinet model can't compete with, like cashew cream sauces and dressings out of tougher ingredients to break down, like ginger. And, of course, I can pull off the exciting trick of creating ice cream out of a frozen banana. The newer models have horsepower like a car and can blend up pretty much anything in about three seconds.

JUICER

The land of at-home juicing is kind of a big deal. I would consider owning a juicer several steps up on the commitment ladder from owning a blender. Juicing takes work. There is the prep of all the produce. You need a lot more kale, spinach, ginger, apple, and carrot than you're going to get in that glass. There is the cleanup of all that leftover pulp, not to mention the machine that needs to be thoroughly washed with all its little parts after each use. So, if you are whipping up your morning wheatgrass shot in your kitchen, or pressing some carrot-apple-ginger midday, you are pretty advanced in your health quest. I'm not trying to scare off the juice-curious. Juicing is loads of fun, and it has a mountain of benefits—but it is work. If you are new to the getting-in-your-kitchen vibe, you may want to start with a few weeks of smoothie making before you run out and get your first juicer.

Of course, if you are psyched for juicing, then run, don't walk to grab your juicer. Juicing is the holy grail of health. It's like getting right to the good stuff, the real deal, the hit of the nutrients directly into your bloodstream. I only warn to get you excited and prepare you for the awesomeness you will experience when you become a full-time juicer. Once you understand and experience the radiant power of juice (especially green juice), the labor that goes into the process will be not only tolerable but enjoyable.

Thankfully, juicers have come a long way, and there are inexpensive models that are relatively easy to clean because they place the pulp neatly in one area. There is the obvious question of what to do with all that pulp. It can feel like a waste throwing away all that fresh produce. There are actually some great recipes out there for using pulp (just Google it), but there are other easier options, including composting, that can use the leftovers in a nice way.

Choosing a Juicer

There are two main types of juicers on the market, and each has its benefits. They're both good options, so you really just need to choose which is best for your life.

CENTRIFUGAL JUICERS: This is the most common type of juicer available. It's the type where you push your fruits and veggies down the top shoot, and then they are sent to a superfast spinning metal blade that separates the juice from the fruit or veggie. Juice comes out a little spout into your cup, and the fruit/veggie pulp goes into a separate container. It's pretty simple and fast to clean. I always grab the pulp and put it through a second time to get a little more juice. The drawback is that the heat generated by the fast-moving blades destroys some of the enzymes in your produce. It also oxidizes the nutrients, lowering the nutritional value of the juice a bit. The machines are usually pretty loud as well, which is fun for waking up the neighbors in the morning. Rise and shine! It's time for juice! This is the type of juicer I have. For me, simplicity counts a ton. Centrifugal juicers are also generally less expensive, so it's easier to recommend them to friends and family without making them think you are nuts.

MASTICATING JUICERS (COLD-PRESS JUICERS): *Cold-pressed* is a buzzword in the juice take-out joints around town. They claim that juice made in this way has more nutrients and is a better quality than juice made by other methods. And they're right. Masticating juicers work by crushing and then pressing your fruits and veggies for the highest yield. Because they don't heat up like the centrifugal models, they do keep more of the fresh nutrients and enzymes from your produce. They also reduce oxidation so your juice will stay fresh for a bit longer, even overnight. But cold-press juicers are a little more pricey and harder to clean. If you get really into your juicing craft, the investment may be worthwhile, but you might want to wait and see just how dedicated to juicing you are before you jump in. Or maybe you can counter your start-up costs by selling your favorite combinations on the sidewalk. Who knows, you could end up with the next big juice empire.

CONTAINERS

A necessary part of any kitchen setup is containers: for oats, noodles, leftovers, and whatever else you may need to store. Again, let's go with what you have. My favorite thing to do is reuse things I already have. Got glass pickle jars, peanut butter containers, and jelly jars staring back at you? Clean them out, get them all shiny, and set them aside. You can bring new life to any container by filling it with lentils, pasta, spices, and more. Plus, when you display what you have in glass, you'll be able to see it, which, for most people, means that you'll remember to use it. It's much easier than when your food is stuffed in boxes and bags that get shoved into your cupboard because they're not pretty.

If you do decide to go out and buy new stuff, make sure you choose materials that don't have harmful chemicals. Glass, ceramic, and stainless steel are safe, but if you must use plastic, make sure to get the most chemical-free versions possible. You will find things labeled as BPA-, PVC-, and phthalate-free, but this doesn't mean they're completely safe. And remember, never use plastic containers in high heat—no microwave, no dishwasher—and recycle them when they get old and scratched.

THIS 'N' THATS

I'm not going to list every piece of kitchen gear you need—that could fill full notebooks—but I do want to mention just a few other things that are necessary and that don't require much explanation. Make sure you have:

MEASURING CUPS: While having both measuring cups for solids and liquids is great, you really only need one set unless you're doing some superprecise baking.

MEASURING SPOONS: You can get these at pretty much any store that has kitchen items. Most grocery stores even have them.

PEELER: Simple, cheap, and found at most stores that have kitchen goods. You can also peel things with a knife; this just makes it easier.

CAN OPENER: Simple, easy, and cheap. We'll be opening a few cans to save time and energy.

Wooden Spoon: These beauties come in handy for stirring boiling foods, and you don't have to worry about nasty chemicals leaching from them.

Slotted Spoon: A great item for pulling out a noodle to test doneness. No, it's not necessary, but it makes life easier.

Metal Spatula: How are you going to get those cookies off your baking sheet without one?

Baking Sheets: Make sure to get ones that don't have those nasty nonstick chemicals.

Colander: Nice metal versions of these are available for relatively cheap.

organize yourself

Okay, now that you have all your goods, it's time to set them up. Before you stuff everything in cupboards, group what goes together. Think of this as a mix between making your kitchen experience more efficient and creating a design. You want your kitchen to look nice, fresh, organized, and pleasing so you are psyched to get in there and create. If we were making a painting, this would be the organizing-brushes phase.

One organizing note: when you're putting your beautiful design together, don't forget about efficiency. If you stack lovely jars too high, you may never get to those lentils in that bottom jar. You want to make things as easy to access as possible.

Save Some Dough

Stocking your kitchen can get expensive if you're not careful,
so if you have to buy any of the more expensive items on this list
(or if you want a fancy upgrade), don't forget to look for used options.
eBay, Craigslist, and even Amazon—not to mention thrift stores and
garage sales—can help you save some serious cashola.

MARKET TIME

Now the superfun part is here: stocking your kitchen with *food*. Time to get your market-ready outfit on and head out to fill up those baskets with yummy goodies. I've prepared a list of easy staples that make a zillion combinations of nutritious and delicious meals for the whole house. Pretty much every time I go to the market, I pick up these same items, and of course, I'm always exploring a few more new things each time to expand and enjoy creative time in the kitchen. If you find me lost in the spice section daydreaming, please say hi and let me know your newest discoveries.

Oh, just a note: make sure you're not starving when you go to the market. It's harder to resist loads of packaged goods and the overbuying of pretty much everything when you're famished and looking at all that food. Make sure you have a meal or a satisfying snack before you head in. A happy belly and calm mind will help you shop from a better place, thus saving wasteful purchases and money.

For the Pantry

Almond butter	Nutritional yeast
Almond milk, unsweetened	Extra virgin olive oil
Cashews, raw, unsalted	Peanut butter
Coconut milk, unsweetened	Quinoa
Coconut oil	Quinoa pasta
Dark chocolate chips	Raw honey
Dijon mustard	Rice and lentils, mixed
Maple syrup, pure	Rice noodles

Produce

Apples	Jalapeños
Avocados	Kale
Bananas	Lemons
Bell peppers	Limes
Blueberries	Red onions
Cucumber	Spinach
Garlic	Strawberries
Ginger	Tomatoes

Spice Cabinet

Cinnamon	Red pepper flakes
Curry powder	Sea salt
Fresh black pepper	Turmeric
Hot sauce	

Schedule It

When I get down to an empty kitchen, I know I need to prioritize hitting the market. If you get into trouble the same way I do, one trick that has worked for me is putting a trip to the market on my calendar. If it's on the schedule, I am much more likely to go than if it's open to "whenever I make time."

These staples aren't super-expensive, and I hope they help rid you of the dreaded concept that eating well has to break the bank. It is not only for those who have a lot of financial wiggle room. And believe me; once you start cooking, you'll use every last bit of these ingredients. Many of them are in a lot of the recipes in this book, and I'm sure that, once you get creative in the kitchen, you'll start inventing ways of your own to use them.

And, yes, I know that these staples aren't the traditional go-to items for many people, but I promise that if you give them a shot and stay with me on our adventure, we'll have an amazing time and you'll feel fantastic from the inside out.

Keeping It Clean

One of the questions that comes up a lot is whether or not you have to eat organic to be healthy. Of course, it would be nice to have everything we consume be 100 percent organic, but ultimately that's not the reality for most of us. Whether it's because of cost or convenience, it's not always possible to have everything in your cart be from a happy local farmer. However, there are ways to prevent disease and achieve radiant health without spending loads of money.

Growing up in the Midwest, we had lots of space for a big garden, and I got my first real-life lesson on keeping our food chemical-free. Growing your own vegetables is the closest thing you can get to local, fresh, and organic, and that's what we did. Cherry tomatoes off the vine are amazing. I grew up loving fresh green peppers more than candy. Our house and garden were surrounded by field after field growing either corn or wheat, depending on the year. Occasionally, a crop-dusting plane would fly by and spray pesticides on a nearby field. I remember watching as the chemicals dropped onto the field, and as the wind blew them over to our garden. My mom would get so mad and yell at the plane, and while it was sad to realize that even the soil not directly being sprayed was getting polluted, I liked watching my mom yell. She was standing up for our rights to grow our own quality food.

Bottom line is we all survived, probably from all the positive vibes of country living, but it's good when you have the option to start with the freshest, cleanest foods possible. Thankfully, the Environmental Working Group has done a lot of the homework for us. They have put together a fantastic list of the Dirty Dozen. Basically, the Dirty Dozen are the 12 foods to buy organic when you can because these items are saturated with chemicals. Logically, this list contains produce that is most exposed and doesn't grow with a protective covering, meaning that we don't peel it; we eat the whole thing. When you pick up these items at your local market or grocery store, please buy organic if at all possible. I say this only because I care. I know it's more expensive, but your health and the health of your family are more than worth it. Also, without dwelling too much on the dark side, you'll save on doctor bills down the line, and the stress and heartache of sickness. Plus, you deserve it.

The Dirty Dozen

Apples   Peaches

Celery   Potatoes

Cherry tomatoes   Snap peas

Cucumbers   Spinach

Grapes   Strawberries

Nectarines   Sweet bell peppers

Also listed for our food education from the Environmental Working Group are the Clean Fifteen, which are okay to eat, even if not organic. This is because they are least likely to hold pesticide residue. Of course, it's better and safer if you try to get organic with most of your produce, but these products, because they have a protective covering, are more free from the chemicals that get sprayed in their direction. They are armed with their shells and are safe for you.

The Clean Fifteen

Asparagus
Avocados
Cabbage
Cantaloupe
Cauliflower
Eggplant
Grapefruit
Kiwis

Mangos
Onions
Papayas
Pineapples
Sweet corn
Sweet peas, frozen
Sweet potatoes

Another thing I often recommend to people who want to eat clean but don't have unlimited funds is to garden, like we did at my house growing up. Not only is it rewarding to grow your own food, but that food is often more delicious. And you don't need a giant space to do this. Even in an apartment you can have a container garden by your window or on your fire escape (just make sure not to impact your escape route).

You can also join a CSA (community-supported agriculture), which provides produce straight from the farm during growing season. You have to pay months before you get the produce, and there's no guarantee that a drought or some other weather problem won't affect yields, but most of the time, these groups provide you with so much fresh food that the cost and risk are worth it.

Finally, go to your local farmers' market. Most of the vendors at these markets work in eco-friendly ways, even if the food isn't certified organic (same with the CSA). You can often get good deals on produce; plus you can live in the joy of knowing that your money is going straight to someone who is caring for the earth and farming in ways that are sustainable.

COOKING UP THE SWEETS

I have some delicious recipes for you in the upcoming pages, but first, a recipe just for you to get you connected to yourself, back in that place of feeling super-awesome. It will help you get excited to get in your kitchen, get creative, and feel fantastic from the inside out. Repeat this recipe twice a day for a month, and you'll be radiating awesomeness from the inside out.

LOVE SAUCE

SERVES 1

1 big handful self-honesty

2 cups self-care

1 tablespoon patience

3 teaspoons attention

Dash of intuition

Soak the honesty in a warm bath of self-care for at least an hour every day. Stir in patience and attention consistently until the mixture is combined evenly. Wait for the right moment and add intuition; you'll know when this is. And then simmer until you feel grounded and inspired. Radiate and Enjoy!

NOW LET'S GET IN THE KITCHEN AND HAVE SOME FUN!

PART
TWO

let
deliciousness
begin

CHAPTER 3

BEVERAGES

blend it; juice it; shake it

Lots of goodness can be delivered in a glass.
Whether it's the comfort of a hot tea to invigorate and ease your mind, a power-packed juice to energize your veins, or a rich smoothie to satisfy and sustain your vibe, the simple contents of a beverage have the potential for brilliance. I hope you enjoy these time-saving, space-creating, heart-warming drinks inspired by a wide range of beauty and cultures from around the world, from my childhood memories on a rural farm, and from the everyday staples of a city kitchen.

JET LAG JUICE

MY job brings me around the world constantly, and the reality is that this is the life I created for myself. I did this with the intention of seeing the world and connecting with hearts and minds along the way. Balancing a proper diet, along with rest and exercise, helps me stay fresh and engaged in whatever time zone I land in. I stumbled upon making this drink one day when I landed back in New York City; this is what was left in my fridge that hadn't gone bad. The kick of ginger blasts out any budding sickness from air travel; and the greens mixed with the citrus and banana give me sustained energy so I can stay in the present moment. A few versions of this supersimple drink have been adopted and are now served by W Hotels, partner gyms, and yoga studios around the world. It's so simple it's silly, but it's just that good.

SERVES 2

1 banana
2 big handfuls spinach
1 cup almond milk
1 cup orange juice
½ inch fresh ginger, peeled
Juice of ½ lime

Blend it.

ENJOY!

DETOX CRAZY KIDS

I'm not a fan of super-extreme detoxes, the kinds where you can't leave your house for days because you're only allowed to suck on a lemon. I'm sure they have their value, but more often I've seen people use them as a quick fix and slide back into bad habits pretty quickly. Here is a light detox drink you can make once or twice a week that will keep your insides and outsides crystal clear and shining bright. I love to make this when I'm back from a long trip. I drink it a few days in a row midmorning or early afternoon in place of that next cup of coffee that I so desperately want. It gives me the boost I need to stay upbeat and have a calm, clear mind to focus on whatever I need to get through that day.

SERVES 2

4 stalks kale, without stems
½ cucumber
1 green apple
Juice of 1 lemon
Juice of 1 lime
2 inches fresh ginger, peeled

Juice it.

ENJOY!

GREEN DREAMS

Green Dreams have become my drinks of choice. A common misconception about starting a healthy lifestyle is that it takes a lot of time, money, and hassle. Those fears don't have a chance with Green Dreams. They're incredibly simple and ridiculously delicious. They leave you fully satisfied and feeling light at the same time. They work for breakfast, as snacks, or as quick boosts. The "Classic" version has become a staple, and adding in local, seasonal, and mood-based ingredients is a fun way to keep things fresh. Green Dreams have become so popular with my friends around the world that several people have added their own touches. I've included a few favorite versions for you to enjoy, as well as the Classic. I hope you love them as much as I do. Cheers.

THE CLASSIC DREAM

SERVES 1

1 banana
1 handful spinach
1 cup almond milk

Blend it.

ENJOY!

SUMMER DREAM

SERVES 1

1 banana
½ cup chopped pineapple
1 handful spinach
1 cup almond milk

Blend it.

ENJOY!

OSCAR'S DREAM

SERVES 1

1 banana

1 handful spinach

1 cup almond milk

1 inch fresh ginger, sliced

Blend it.

ENJOY!

MOTHER MARY

Every once in a while, I order tomato juice on an airplane because somehow
it seems like the right thing to do when at 30,000 feet. Each time I drink a can of the slightly processed
stuff, my imagination wanders about how I can improve this classic in my own kitchen. Back on land,
I started experimenting, tossing in spices and veggies. With the help of a few surprise ingredients, I
landed on a staple that has me drinking up the tomato goodness.

SERVES 1

3 tomatoes
2 stalks celery
Juice of 1 lime
Juice of 1 lemon
½ jalapeño
8 shakes hot sauce
2 teaspoons horseradish
1 inch fresh-cut ginger
1 teaspoon maple syrup
½ teaspoon sea salt
½ teaspoon black pepper

Blend it.

Chill in the fridge until cold, about 2 hours.

ENJOY!

ISLAND TIME SHAKE-ME-UP

This creamy delight is inspired by my friend Erna Malia from Malaysia.

We met when I was leading a class on a helipad. She was all smiles with great energy, and I immediately wanted to be friends with her. Her head and arms were covered to observe her religion, and she sported a T-shirt from my Reebok collaboration that said, "Make Your Own Yoga." I knew this lady was cool, and I was excited to get to know her more. She brought me a cookbook she had put together of her favorite recipes inspired by my blog. This was one of her favorites. I added maple syrup. Her recipe asked for 2 tablespoons of condensed milk and 1 tablespoon of chocolate sauce instead of coconut milk. Enjoy whichever way you like best.

SERVES 2

1 ripe avocado, pitted and sliced
½ cup coconut milk
1 tablespoon raw cacao
1 tablespoon maple syrup

Blend it.

ENJOY!

OH BERRY

This antioxidant treat is amazing. Thanks to the trusty lime tree I received as a gift from my friend Marina from Russia, I have an ample supply of limes to play around with in many dishes and drinks. Marina has a great way with growing plants and has inspired me to be more natural when it comes to remembering there are lots of things we can grow if we just take the time and attention. She's a gardening genius, and while she teaches me a few words of Russian each day, she tells stories about growing food in her yard as a young girl in Russia. It was a practical and inexpensive way for her family to eat. Oh Berry isn't your average berry smoothie; it's injected with love from Russia.

SERVES 2

1 cup strawberries
1 cup blueberries
1 cup orange juice
Juice of ½ lime
¼ cup coconut milk
1 teaspoon cinnamon (optional)

Blend it.

Sprinkle cinnamon on top for an extra-fancy look.

ENJOY!

COCO-CHOCOLATE SHAKE

Coconut milk has become one of my at-home staples of creation. Some people go to lentils, grains, or pasta; I go to coconut milk. Whether serving as a foundation, mixer, or creamy enhancer, I love the versatility and fresh flavor that coconut milk offers so many dishes.

When thinking of a chocolate milkshake, the first thing that comes to my mind is *yes, please*, and the second thing to come to mind is *ouch*. Whether because of a brain freeze or bellyache, we sometimes gain a whole lot of discomfort from our traditional milkshake friend. This version is friendlier on the belly and tastes superfresh and amazing. I hope you love it as much as I do.

SERVES 2

1 frozen banana* or 1 nonfrozen banana and 6 ice cubes

1½ cup coconut milk

1 ounce cut dark chocolate

1 tablespoon raw cacao

1 tablespoon maple syrup

Blend it.

ENJOY!

* Make sure to peel the banana before you freeze it.

CRUNCH AND STORMY

while I was growing up, after a big dance recital or basketball game, we would go out for ice cream. I think the trend these days may have evolved into going out for a healthy juice or smoothie. Better for the health of kids, maybe, but going out for ice cream was so much fun. As part social gathering of friends and part delicious treat, I've updated one of my favorite ice cream treats into a healthier version that is kid and adult friendly.

SERVES 2

1 frozen banana* or 1 nonfrozen banana and 6 ice cubes
1 cup coconut milk
1 chocolate chip cookie, crumbled
1 tablespoon chocolate sauce (or ½ ounce melted dark chocolate)

Blend it.

ENJOY!

* Make sure to peel the banana before you freeze it.

WATERMELON SPLASH

On the superhot days of summer, during my childhood in Illinois, we would hang out in the yard, eat watermelon, and get all sticky. It usually worked to cool us off and was a whole lot of fun. My earliest memory of this tradition was when I was about 3 years old; I stood on a big tire that was in the yard, enjoying my slice, and I accidentally swallowed a seed. I was convinced that I was going to grow a watermelon in my belly. Terrified, I told my mom that she needed to get it out of my belly. She assured me I would only grow a watermelon in my belly if I ate a whole bunch of dirt and drank a lot of water. That confused me a little, but I finally settled down. Now I sit on my front porch (fire escape) in New York City and enjoy my Watermelon Splash with no fear, even if I do swallow a seed now and then.

SERVES 2

3 cups fresh-cut watermelon
1 cup orange juice
2 inches sliced fresh ginger
½ cup fresh mint leaves

Blend it.

ENJOY!

APANGO TANGO

Short, simple, and sweet. Sometimes, when there are just a few pieces of fruit lying around that you don't expect to go together, something good can happen. It's like a culture clash in fashion: mixing stripes with a bright pattern. I like that kind of thing in expressing myself with what I wear, and sometimes it works with food, too. The worst-case situation when combining great foods is that you don't like the combination, but the foods are still great to enjoy. Luckily this combo didn't fall prey to that; it turned out great. I hope you enjoy.

SERVES 2

1 apple
1 mango
2 cups coconut water
1 inch fresh ginger, peeled

Blend it.

ENJOY!

COLD BUSTER

This drink takes some bravery. It's spicy. It's intense. It's wild. It will bust through an existing cold and prevent the threat of one. If you get supercourageous, down this once a week as a preventative and feat of exhilaration. The great news is it works and will clear your pipes, lungs, throat, and foggy brain. When you drink it and are already feeling in tip-top shape, you will sky-rocket to a superhuman state of focused attention.

SERVES 1

1 orange, peeled
1 lemon, peeled
1 inch fresh-cut turmeric
2 inches fresh-cut ginger
1 teaspoon cayenne pepper
2 shakes hot sauce
1 clove garlic, mashed

Blend all ingredients with 1 cup water.

ENJOY!

MELTDOWN TEA

This calming tea is inspired by my friend Suraya Sam. We met in New York City originally at Strala, and then again in Singapore, where she is from. Suraya has developed namastéas, her own blend of calming teas. We all have meltdowns, and when they are happening, nothing seems to be able to fix them. Meltdown Tea is my answer to all the problems that feel overwhelming, but that I know will pass once I relax and find a clear solution. The process of making the tea is just as therapeutic as sipping it. I hope this tea eases your meltdowns into happy, calm places for you. Thanks, Suraya.

SERVES 2

2 inches sliced fresh ginger
½ cup mint leaves
1 teaspoon cinnamon

Boil 4 cups of water with ginger.

Add mint leaves and simmer for 5 minutes covered.

Pour into a mug and top with cinnamon.

ENJOY!

NEVER-GET-SICK TEA

This tea was inspired by my friend Jaya, who spent a few months in New York City at Strala. She spent a lot of her non-yoga time cooking for all her new friends. Her heart is huge and her cooking skills are massive. She didn't make this tea for me, but I was motivated to explore in my kitchen one day after hanging around her at the studio and listening to her boast about the healing power of turmeric and ginger. I went home and boiled some up. It's supersimple but amazing. It's also a great midday coffee substitute to keep the energy going without the crazy effect of another cup of coffee.

SERVES 2

2 inches fresh ginger, sliced
1 inch fresh turmeric, sliced
1 teaspoon cinnamon (optional)

Boil 4 cups of water.

Add ginger and turmeric, and simmer for 5 minutes.

Top with cinnamon if you're feeling extra-fancy.

ENJOY!

FIRE ESCAPE TEA

I discovered this physically and emotionally cooling drink one day after realizing that I had been consuming way too many iced coffees in the months of June, July, and August. Growing up, my mom would always put a big glass jar outside on the front steps with a few tea bags, and we'd have iced tea in a few hours. I adopted that concept in a New York City way: Fire Escape Tea.

This version is infused with mint, lemon, and lime to spruce it up and make it a little special for when guests come over. I like to use green tea; it's a crowd favorite.

SERVES 6

2 tablespoons loose green tea
½ cup lavender leaves
1 cup mint leaves
Juice of 1 lemon
Juice of 1 lime

Pour 2 quarts of water into a glass pitcher.

Add the tea, lavender, and mint to a wire mesh strainer and place in water.

Sit the pitcher on a sunny window ledge or outside for 1 to 2 hours. Your tea will be ready when the water is a darker color.

Add lemon and lime juice to the water.

Slice lemons and limes, and add slices to the pitcher.

Serve over ice.

ENJOY!

HOT HOT CHOCOLATE

Hot chocolate is one of my all-time favorite comfort drinks. When I was growing up, we made hot chocolate on the stove or in the microwave with milk and a couple tablespoons of Ovaltine. I was into it, but I saw more potential. For me, it doesn't have to be a winter wonderland to enjoy the richness and creaminess of hot chocolate. I like this drink as an after-dinner dessert or midafternoon snack year-round.

My artist and Strala friend Renata Rucka, known as Pia Brunost online, lives surrounded by nature, snow, and mountains in Norway, and she has spruced up my traditional hot chocolate with a few special ingredients. Her meals are always inspired and seem to be conversing with the nature that surrounds her. I feel these special ingredients will hopefully turn you from an occasional hot chocolate dabbler to a fancy hot chocolate connoisseur.

SERVES 2

4 cups almond milk

3 ounces dark chocolate

2 shakes hot sauce

1 pinch ground cayenne

1 pinch ground cinnamon

Combine almond milk and chocolate in a medium saucepan over medium heat.

Stir constantly until chocolate is melted.

Add hot sauce and mix well.

Remove from the heat and top with cayenne and cinnamon.

CHAPTER 4

BREAKFAST
morning magic

It can happen slow or fast. It can happen in a feast or in just a couple of bites. It can be a drink, a jolt, or skipped entirely. Breakfast comes in many shapes and forms for each of us. Depending on the day, the schedule, and our needs, breakfast has the ability to set us up for the rest of our day. I'll be honest; my ideal breakfast is the Classic Green Dream paired with something delicious and nutritious, like avocado on toast, but oftentimes, breakfast is a cup of coffee on the go. On those days, fuzzy brain creeps in midmorning, and I am reminded to make more space and time for proper nourishment. It really doesn't have to take that long.

It feels indulgent to take the time to create and enjoy a breakfast that fits on a plate instead of in a cup or mug. When I make the time to put together an actual meal for breakfast, I feel super-fueled up for the day and ready to get out there and enjoy the magic. When we run on fumes, it's trickier to see the magic that is in store for us each day, so fuel up properly more often than not and enjoy feeling fantastic from the inside out. Incorporate some full plates with your morning routine and you'll see how energized you can be. Get your proper plates and bowls ready; it's time for a hearty breakfast.

TOFU VEGGIE SCRAMBLE

A nice big plate of steamy veggie scramble is one of my favorite nourishing comfort foods. On a recent trip to the W Hotel in Vieques, Puerto Rico, I got the pleasure of learning some of Chef Fernando's trade secrets in the kitchen. I got super-inspired by his spin of fresh veggies with a local spicy island twist. I have great memories of hanging out in the kitchen playing the role of sous chef, adding in every variety of vegetable we could find, messing around with different spices, and even learning his patient technique of adding a little liquid and letting it all simmer and soak up the flavors, which makes the dish superspecial and really delicious.

SERVES 2

2 tablespoons olive oil

1 onion, diced

1 potato, diced

2 tomatoes, sliced

5 shitake mushrooms, sliced

7 ounces firm tofu, chopped

1 avocado, pitted and sliced

1 pinch sea salt

1 teaspoon red pepper flakes

Place the oil in a skillet over medium heat.

Add the onion and potato. Stir with a spatula and cook until the onion is browned.

Add the tomatoes and mushrooms. Stir for 3 minutes.

Add 2 tablespoons of water and cook down for 3 minutes until the sauce thickens.

Add the tofu and avocado.

Cook and stir constantly for 4 or 5 minutes until everything looks combined and yummy.

Toss in the sea salt and red pepper flakes over everything and stir for one last time.

Remove from the heat and serve.

ENJOY!

RANCHEROS

One of my favorite diners in New York City is Café Habana. The food is really good and unpretentious. The atmosphere is cool. The restaurant is basically a trailer with some bar stools and a few tables. If you are lucky enough to get a spot inside, you will feel like you got into the most chill, in-the-know party. I love its Huevos Rancheros so much that I try to re-create it at home without the eggs and some extra veggies. I get pretty close, and it's nice to enjoy, but it's always a special treat getting a spot at the bar for a little New York City Cuban experience.

SERVES 2

2 tablespoons olive oil

1 onion, chopped

2 roma or heirloom tomatoes, chopped

½ jalapeño, chopped

2 cloves garlic, smashed

2 cups black beans

1 pinch sea salt

7 ounces firm tofu

2 corn tortillas

Juice of 1 lime

¼ cup fresh cilantro

1 shake hot sauce

Place 1 tablespoon of olive oil in a skillet over medium heat.

Add the onion, tomatoes, jalapeño, and 1 clove of garlic.

Stir and cook for 3 to 5 minutes. Remove from the heat and set aside.

Add the beans to the skillet with the remaining clove of garlic and sea salt. Cook for 5 minutes or until warm all the way through.

In a second skillet, add the remaining tablespoon of olive oil and tofu. Cook until warmed through.

Add the tofu to the rest of your mixture in the first skillet.

Place tortillas in the second skillet and heat for a few moments until they are warm.

Transfer the warm tortillas to a plate. Add the beans, tofu, and tomato salsa to each tortilla. Top with lime juice, cilantro, and hot sauce.

ENJOY!

PEAR PILE-UP

I love to play around with a few simple ingredients to see how magically delicious the combination can turn out. My scrappy nature, along with interest in design and diverse cultures, has led to some quirky combos on the home front. My time in the kitchen often gives my mind a break, and I can let intuition purely take over. The Pear Pile-Up revealed itself to me upon returning from a long trip while scavenging for what was still edible in my kitchen. I hope you enjoy this scrumptious sculpture; let your inner Picasso play today.

SERVES 1

1 pear, sliced

2 tablespoons peanut butter

½ cup raisins

1 apple, sliced

1 tablespoon strawberry jam

½ cup sliced almonds

1 teaspoon cinnamon

1 tablespoon honey

Pile the pear slices with the peanut butter, raisins, apple slices, jam, almonds, peanut butter, more pear slices, and so on, towering high with your own creative combinations. Top with the cinnamon and honey. Serve on a plate with a fork.

ENJOY!

SMILEY TOAST

I don't think I'll ever grow up, and I'm fine with that. Sometimes, I just want to have chocolate for breakfast, and I have to laugh myself into eating fruits. I created a smiley face in my toast one day, and it helped me get some extra nutrients and antioxidants as well as my creamy chocolate fix. I'm sure this breakfast will convince kids to eat fruits in the morning, but it works for adults, too!

SERVES 1

2 slices bread

2½ tablespoons chocolate almond butter

½ banana, sliced

1 cup blueberries

2 strawberries, sliced lengthwise

Toast the bread and spread with the chocolate almond butter.

Place two banana slices on each piece of toast. Top the banana slices with blueberries to form the eyes.

Arrange the remaining banana for the nose and add the strawberries for the mouth.

ENJOY!

HASH BROWNS

Growing up, on the rare occasion when my mom wasn't available to make dinner, we had Dad doing his thing in the kitchen. My brother and I would get a little scared, but it was like an adventure watching him try to whip up some nourishment for us.

My dad is the best at making what he likes to eat, which is true for most of us, and for him that's eggs, toast, and hash browns. Everything is usually burned, and I'm still not sure if he likes it best this way or if that's just how it has always turned out. Either way, hash browns make me nostalgic for the rare Dinners by Dad. I like to eat my hash browns in the evenings. You can take yours whenever you like, of course. This recipe is slightly different from Dad's. I've experimented a bit to get a gooier updated version.

SERVES 2

2 red potatoes, peeled and chopped

2 teaspoons curry powder

1 teaspoon black pepper

1 teaspoon red pepper flakes

1 pinch sea salt

2 tablespoons butter

½ onion, chopped

1 teaspoon hot sauce

Boil the red potatoes until softened, about 15 minutes. Drain and cut the potatoes into smaller pieces.

Combine the potatoes with the spices and mix well.

Add 1 tablespoon butter and onion to a skillet, and cook over medium heat.

Add the potatoes to the skillet and mix well.

Form 2 pancakes with the potatoes and flatten with a spatula.

Cook on medium to low heat for 5 to 8 minutes until one side is browned.

Remove from the heat. Add the remaining butter to the skillet. Place the pancakes back in the skillet on the other side.

Cook on medium to low heat for 5 to 8 minutes.

Remove from the heat. Top with the hot sauce and serve.

ENJOY!

FIT ELVIS

The king of rock, the inventor of pop, the star who defined how to be cool: Elvis. We love to remember him as vibrant and full of energy. We also can't ignore the dark side and the decline of his vitality. We all have our heroes that we had hoped we could have helped along the way, and millions would have loved to have helped Elvis take better care of himself during the time he started slipping. But we can see an opportunity, too, to help ourselves when we witness poor choices that others make and the consequences of those choices. We can honor his spirit, talent, and the energy he left with us through song and dance and passion in so many ways. I love to honor the king of rock by making my adapted version of his famous fried peanut butter and banana sandwich. It's a bit healthier, of course, and I like to dance to "Jailhouse Rock" cranked up on high volume when I make it. Join me for a fun adventure in celebrating rock 'n' roll and our vibrant potential. Make good choices, kids!

SERVES 1

2 tablespoons almond butter

2 slices rye bread

1 banana

1 teaspoon cinnamon

1 tablespoon nondairy butter

Spread the almond butter on 1 slice of bread.

Slice the banana and add the slices to the bread.

Top with ½ teaspoon cinnamon.

Place the nondairy butter in a skillet over medium heat.

Place the second slice of bread over the other to make your sandwich.

Place the sandwich in the skillet and cook for 5 to 8 minutes until golden brown.

Flip the sandwich and cook the other side for 5 more minutes.

Remove from the heat and top with the remaining cinnamon.

ENJOY!

RED-PEPPER POSH TOAST

When you move to a big city from a small town, you find some simple things that can be made fancy. Entire cafés dedicated to peanut butter or cupcakes and fancy ways to prepare toast would be crazy in my hometown, but they're the norm in New York City. The crazes and fads always teach you something, and they provide many delicious treats to sample. In the case of fancy things on toast, I got suckered into spending more cash on a piece of toast than several loafs of bread a few times and enjoyed some incredibly yummy creations. Hearing my mom's voice in my head, *You know you can make that at home,* got me thinking, *Hey, I should try to make this at home.* Well, I went for it, and changed it up a bit, too, adding my own dash of creativity, and it turned out pretty tasty. This is my version of a once-purchased posh piece of toast in SoHo. I hope you enjoy the DIY version at a fraction of the cost.

SERVES 1

2 slices bread

2 tablespoons red-pepper paste

1 teaspoon hot sauce

1 clove garlic

1 tablespoon olive oil

1 roma tomato

1 handful fresh basil leaves

1 pinch sea salt

Toast the bread.

Blend the red-pepper paste, hot sauce, garlic, ½ tablespoon olive oil, and tomato.

Spread the mixture on the toast. Add the basil leaves and drizzle with the remaining olive oil.

Top with the sea salt.

ENJOY!

TOFU TOAST

Upon discovering the world of fancy toast, I imagined the endless possibilities of healthy foods to eat on toast. I like sweet. I like savory. I like spicy. I like it all. If it tastes good, I'm in, and if it's healthy and yummy, I'll put it into the usual rotation. With all the travel I do, my on-the-road breakfasts are limited to some fresh fruit or a smoothie, if I'm lucky. Airport breakfast can be pretty brutal, but I know where to hunt for healthy snacks, or, better yet, I bring along a banana and some mixed nuts for energy to last until lunchtime. Airport travel can bring out some pretty bad eating habits. It often feels like an in-between zone where, if you eat junk, it doesn't count, because you're not really home or at your destination. Limbo land. The line for fast food is stacked long for that quick-fix breakfast sandwich. I know better than to put all that processed stuff in my body, but I can definitely see the allure. The smell, taste, and texture appeal to the comfort that we crave when we are on the road. This Tofu Toast is inspired to fulfill those fast-food pleasure centers without any of the unhealthy effects.

SERVES 1

1 tablespoon nondairy butter

¼ red onion

1 clove garlic

4 ounces firm tofu, chopped

¼ red bell pepper, chopped

1 handful cherry tomatoes, sliced in half

¼ jalapeño, chopped

Juice of ½ lime

1 teaspoon chili powder

1 teaspoon red pepper flakes

1 tablespoon almond or coconut milk

1 tablespoon nutritional yeast

2 slices bread

½ tablespoon maple syrup (optional)

Sauté the nondairy butter, onion, and garlic in a skillet over medium heat.

Mix the tofu, bell pepper, tomatoes, jalapeño, lime juice, and spices in a medium bowl with a fork.

Add in the milk and nutritional yeast.

Pour the mixture into a skillet and cook for 5 to 8 minutes, stirring occasionally.

Toast the bread.

Add the cooked tofu mixture to the toast.

Top with the maple syrup, if using.

ENJOY!

BANANA-ALMOND BUTTER PANCAKES

Pancakes have the vibe of extreme leisure on a lazy weekend morning.
When I was growing up, we sometimes had pancakes for dinner, which was superfun. Probably one of the few vegetarian meals we would have. And it was mostly just that my mom didn't want to take the time to pressurize a roast or cook something all day. I wasn't a fan of eating meat, so pancake dinners were the top in my book. These days, my weekends are usually jam-packed with Strala, travel, and other activities, so lazy weekend days are mostly alive in my imagination. But why miss out on pancakes just because of a normal busy weekend schedule? I keep pancake dinners on rotation. This version is superyummy and also nourishing.

SERVES 2

1 tablespoon sugar

1 tablespoon brown sugar

2 cups almond flour

2½ teaspoons baking powder

½ teaspoon sea salt

2 bananas

3 egg replacers

2 tablespoons almond butter

4 tablespoons nondairy butter

1½ cups almond milk

½ teaspoon vanilla extract

½ cup sliced almonds

1 tablespoon olive oil

1 teaspoon powdered sugar

1 tablespoon maple syrup

Whisk together the sugar, brown sugar, flour, baking powder, and sea salt.

Mash the bananas, and combine with the egg replacers and almond butter.

Add half of the banana mixture to the flour-and-sugar mixture.

Blend in the nondairy butter, almond milk, and vanilla.

Fold in half of the sliced almonds.

In a medium skillet, add the olive oil.

Using a ladle, pour the pancake mixture onto the skillet to form medium pancakes.

Cook for 2 minutes on each side.

Remove from the heat.

Top with the remaining sliced almonds, bananas, the powdered sugar, and the maple syrup.

ENJOY!

AÇAÍ BOWL

This recipe comes from another Russian friend in my life. Ksenia Avdulova

came into Strala for class, and I noticed her determination on the mat right away and wanted to know more about her. It wasn't surprising to find out that she was an entrepreneur following her passion of superfoods, photography, and sharing the message of superfood powers. Ksenia came over one morning to make breakfast before Strala classes and test me out on superfoods. It was my first time eating an açaí bowl, and I have to admit that I felt a bit charged up, like a superhero. Açaí is a traditional Brazilian superfood treat, and can be found in most health-food stores as a puree in smoothie packs. It's crazy flexible as a base for loads of happy breakfast variations. I've tried this with lots of different combos, and it always turns out yummy and fills me with Wonder Woman strength.

SERVES 2

2 packs unsweetened açaí puree

¼ cup blackberries

¼ cup blueberries

1 banana

½ cup spinach

½ avocado, pitted and sliced

1 tablespoon cinnamon

1 cup coconut water

¼ cup granola

¼ cup goji berries

¼ cup coconut chips

1 tablespoon maca (optional)

Blend the açaí puree, berries, banana, spinach, avocado, cinnamon, coconut water, and maca, if using.

Top with the granola, goji berries, and coconut chips.

ENJOY!

BANANA BOAT

I have vivid memories of coming home on the school bus from kindergarten when my mom had prepared a midafternoon snack: a banana-boat sandwich with a side of applesauce and cottage cheese. I remember being tuckered out after school, and how the banana boat would bring me back to life and give me energy to make it through the rest of the day. I now enjoy an updated version for breakfast, lunch, or as a post-yoga snack. It serves the same purpose of bringing my energy back up to excited.

SERVES 1

1 banana
1 slice bread
2 tablespoons peanut butter

1 tablespoon strawberry jam
1 teaspoon cinnamon

Peel the banana and place on the bread.

Spread the peanut butter on the banana.

Spread the jam on top of the peanut butter.

Top with the cinnamon.

Fold the bread into a boat.

ENJOY!

COCONUT PARFAIT

While leading a retreat at the W Hotel in the Maldives, the chef prepared delicious and nourishing recipes inspired by my book *Make Your Own Rules Diet*. The chef added quite a few local, island-themed touches that gave me some new tricks to take home, try out, and share. This breakfast (and almost dessert) is such a delicious treat to start the day with. It doesn't take long to prepare, but you have to start on this recipe the night before for the parfait to set up properly. Don't worry: it only takes a few minutes, and you'll have a fresh breakfast waiting for you in the morning. I enjoyed this after many sunrise yoga sessions, and it kept me going strong until refueling after a swim in the ocean or dip in the pool. It works to refresh and start the day when I'm back to city life, as well.

SERVES 2

1 cup coconut milk

4 tablespoons chia seeds

1 teaspoon vanilla extract

5 tablespoons granola

1 cup fresh strawberries and
   blueberries

Combine the coconut milk, chia seeds, and vanilla.

Stir and cover. Refrigerate for at least 8 hours.

Remove the mixture in the morning and combine with the granola and fresh berries.

ENJOY!

GRANDMA'S FRUIT SALAD

My grandma always has a giant Tupperware bowl of ready-to-serve fruit salad. I've noticed over the years that it gets better the longer it sets, and is best on day two. I've found a way to re-create this two-day fruit salad perfection on day one by adding some secret ingredients. Grandma's version is supersimple: dump several cans of fruit in a big bowl; serve. Mine is a tad more complex. Grandma is super-efficient and has a lot of people to feed all the time. I'm not taking care of as many yet, so I can take my time with this one.

SERVES 4

2 cups strawberries, sliced

2 cups blueberries

1 cup raspberries

1 cup blackberries

2 cups seedless grapes

Juice of 2 oranges

2 peaches, sliced

1 pear, sliced

Juice of 4 limes

Juice of 2 lemons

1 cup seltzer water

1 tablespoon cinnamon

Combine all the ingredients in a large bowl and mix well.

Refrigerate until ready to serve.

ENJOY!

CHAPTER 5

SNACKS
munchy madness

Snacks can save the day, literally. When I'm not on the road, I spend a good amount of time like many of us do: office style. I can go for hours and hours getting through planning, organizing, and creating. As the time flies by, hunger sets in, and I know drinking another cup of coffee isn't the best solution. I've come up with a few midday savers that keep my brain feeling fresh and clear to tackle whatever I'd like to accomplish, and my body feeling energized and vibrant to make it to the next meal. Snack on the good stuff and you'll get more done with less effort.

OLIVE GUACAMOLE

Guacamole is one of those things that is so easy to buy, but almost as easy to make fresh. In my usual fashion of using what I have around the house to make something (hopefully) edible, I uncovered this repeatable and yummy guacamole recipe with extra olive goodness.

SERVES 3

2 avocados

½ cup chopped onion

½ cup mixed green and black olives, chopped

¼ cup olive juice

½ tomato, diced

2 cloves garlic, minced

4 shakes hot sauce

1 teaspoon red pepper flakes

1 teaspoon chili flakes

Juice of ½ lemon

Juice of ½ lime

Mash the avocados with a fork in a small bowl, and stir in the onion, olives, olive juice, tomato, garlic, hot sauce, and spices.

Toss in the lemon and lime juices, and mash them in with a fork.

ENJOY!

PINEAPPLE SALSA

Salsa is one of those things I feel funny about buying. I know I can make it at home easily, but I feel strangely compelled to and captivated by the salsa section of the market. There are so many varieties that it's like a whole world, and I have to confess that I've purchased loads of jars over the years. Thankfully, the glass jars make handy containers for all kinds of things, including my own salsa inventions. In New York City, we see trends explode quickly, sometimes staying and sometimes fading. I'd be game to frequent a salsa bar (if one ever popped up) to try out multiple varieties, flavors, creative additions, and levels of spiciness in one sitting. A favorite addition that I've settled on is pineapple, which gives sweetness to a full-bodied, spicy salsa. Get out your veggie chips and dig in!

SERVES 2

2 tomatoes, diced

1 cup chopped pineapple

½ red onion, diced

1 clove garlic, mashed

Juice of 1 lime

4 shakes hot sauce

1 teaspoon chili flakes

1 teaspoon black pepper

1 pinch sea salt

Blend lightly.

ENJOY!

BEET CRISPS

I love salty almost as much as I love sweet. I don't want to have to pick just one favorite, though. With chips, it's impossible to eat just one, so why not find a healthier version to enjoy a satisfying amount without a bellyache or any guilt? The hot-pink color of a beet is just so incredible. The benefits are massive and diverse. Beets contain a big dose of vitamins A, B, and C, and are great for lowering blood pressure, boosting stamina, fighting inflammation, and acting as a natural cleanser for the body by supporting detoxification.

SERVES 4

2 tablespoons olive oil

1 tablespoon maple syrup

2 beets, thinly sliced

1 teaspoon sea salt

1 teaspoon black pepper

Preheat the oven to 350 degrees Fahrenheit.

Combine the olive oil and maple syrup in a small bowl.

Dip the sliced beets in the olive oil mixture and blot off the excess moisture.

Line a baking sheet with parchment paper. Place the beet slices on the lined sheet and bake for 25 minutes or until crisp.

Remove from the heat and let cool for 5 minutes.

Sprinkle with the sea salt and pepper.

ENJOY!

TANYA'S KALE KRUNCH

A raw diet has the potential to prevent and heal an incredible number of diverse health and energy problems. My friend Tanya is proof of that healing power. Not only has she empowered herself with a raw diet, but she has created an awesome café, Tanya's, in the heart of London. It's helped make eating raw superhip and fun, bringing radiance to the United Kingdom one dish at a time. I had the pleasure of soaking up every last bit of Tanya's uniquely flavorful kale chips one late night in London as the kitchen was closing, and I had to bug her for the recipe so I could enjoy it over and over again at home. I know you will adore her special spin on this healthy classic.

SERVES 2

1 cup cashews

1 bunch kale, stems removed

2 tablespoons lemon juice

1 tablespoon tahini

½ red bell pepper, deseeded and chopped

2 tablespoons nutritional yeast

1 teaspoon Himalayan salt

1 clove garlic

Soak the cashews in 1 cup water for at least 2 hours. Drain after soaking.

Roughly chop the kale.

Blend the cashews with a ½ cup fresh water, lemon juice, and tahini.

Add the remaining ingredients and blend until smooth.

Pour the sauce over the kale and use your hands to massage it all over the greens.

Arrange the kale on dehydrator sheets and let dehydrate for 10 hours at 110 degrees Fahrenheit.

Store in an airtight container or in a sealable plastic bag to keep the kale chips crunchy.

ENJOY!

MANGO SALSA

Supersimple, fresh, and light for summer or anytime of the year when you feel like a sweet and savory light salad. This is a favorite of my friend Erna from Malaysia. It's a staple in her weekly rotation to beat the pulsing heat of the city of Kuala Lumpur. I have added a few more of my favorite veggies to make this into more of a sustainable midday meal or hearty snack. It's so simple and yummy, and allows for the freedom to add whatever veggies you like best. Fresh, crunchy veggies work best in this delightful dish.

SERVES 4

1 small green mango, chopped

5 shallots, chopped

2 tomatoes, chopped

2 jalapeños, chopped

Juice of 1 lime

Juice of ½ lemon

1 teaspoon sea salt

Combine everything. Mix and mash with a fork, and serve as a dip with chips or veggies.

ENJOY!

TREE-POSE POUCH

This tasty snack has been my savior on those days of being on the go around town. Whether I'm traveling for the entire day or running around the city working on projects, having a Tree-Pose Pouch has been my quirky sidekick that also is good for sharing. When we're kids, it's normal to have a snack packed along with us for the day. Somehow, we have fallen out of the habit as adults. Join me in bringing a healthy snack along with you for your action-packed days. We'll get a lot more done, be able to focus for longer, and not be subject to needing to refuel with unhealthy office snacks or loads of caffeine.

SERVES 1

2 cups oats

1 cup mixed nuts, chopped

1 apple, chopped

¼ cup dark chocolate chips

¼ cup raisins

1 teaspoon cinnamon

1 teaspoon cardamom

¼ cup maple syrup

⅛ cup coconut oil

Preheat the oven to 350 degrees Fahrenheit.

Combine the oats, nuts, apple, chocolate, and raisins in a large bowl. Add the cinnamon, cardamom, maple syrup, and coconut oil. Mix well.

Spread the mixture on a cookie sheet and bake for 30 minutes. Remove from the heat and allow the mixture to cool.

ENJOY!

AVOCADO-CASHEW CREAM DIP

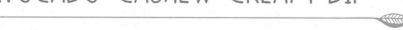

Once I had started playing around with making my own dressings, I couldn't stop. I began accumulating lots of little glass jars full of my creations. On one dressing jam session, I took a taste and found a recipe that was too thick and creamy to use as a salad dressing, but it worked wonders as a spread for toast, sandwiches, or as a straight-up veggie dip. Once I took a dive into avocado-cashew cream, my mind-body connection exploded with excitement. I hope yours does, too.

SERVES 2

1 avocado, pitted and sliced

¼ cup cashews

½ cup coconut milk

1 tablespoon nutritional yeast

1 teaspoon red pepper flakes

1 teaspoon turmeric

5 shakes hot sauce

1 pinch sea salt

2 cloves garlic (optional)

Blend all the ingredients.

Use them as a dip with veggies or a spread on toast.

ENJOY!

PARADISE ISLAND DIP

This recipe found its way to me through an exploration of leftovers in my kitchen that had been waiting for me to return from Bali to fully appreciate its vibrancy and potential. This same trip to Bali to lead a retreat had been incredibly energizing in a way that I hadn't been expecting. I think it had a lot to do with the strength of the ocean and the massive size of the waves crashing in. You couldn't help but be charged up by the power of the current. The air was so fresh and invigorating.

The Balinese culture of extreme friendliness can be almost comical to an urban Westerner. I dare you to try to be the last person to say thank-you to anyone in Bali. The Balinese will always trump you with a thank-you to the point that you can make a fun game out of it: "No, thank you." "No, thank you." "Thank you." "Thank you." It's the gratitude game of belly laughs. The food I had enjoyed was a lot of fresh fruits, veggies, and spices that I'm sure were enhanced by my electrified mood.

The creaminess is super-indulgent, and the spice and freshness keep the dip light and interesting. I hope you enjoy my Bali discovery as much as I have.

SERVES 4

½ cup coconut or almond milk

1 red or orange bell pepper

1 tablespoon Dijon mustard

1 tablespoon olive oil

1 teaspoon red pepper flakes

1 teaspoon chili powder

1 teaspoon tomato paste

1 pinch sea salt

1 pinch black pepper

Blend and serve with veggies or chips.

ENJOY!

CHEESY SAUCE

Cheese sauce sounds so yummy, rich, and comforting, but it may not leave such a good feeling too soon after indulging. I've got a recipe that is much easier on the system than a traditional cheese sauce, and hopefully it will leave you feeling just as great after you eat it. I have this one in regular rotation for dipping veggies and chips. I've also used it as a pasta sauce and in casseroles. You can get as creative as you like. This cheese sauce has serious range.

SERVES 2

1 cup cashews

½ cup almond milk

¼ cup nutritional yeast

1 teaspoon red pepper flakes

1 tablespoon Dijon mustard

4 shakes hot sauce

Blend and serve as a dip for your veggies or chips.

ENJOY!

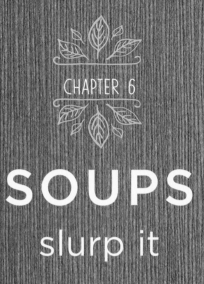

CHAPTER 6

SOUPS

slurp it

I've always been a soup person, probably because
I grew up with some master soup makers. Between my grandmas, aunts, and mom, we had loads of nutritious and wholesome
soups to keep our minds clear and calm and our bodies strong
and nourished. My love of soup has continued to simmer since
I've moved into a kitchen space that inspires me. Even when
I was in my first apartment in New York City, a whopping 200
square feet of my own sanctuary, I played around with my two
little burners and minifridge and a few ingredients I'd picked
up at the market. Back in those days I made up something
I called DIY Sushi Soup. It wasn't so spectacular to include
as a full recipe here, but I mention it to give you an idea
of where my mind was. I included water, rice, spinach, and

soy and hot sauces; sort of boiled everything together for a while; and simmered it until it smelled like a meal. I survived, and my skills have thankfully improved and expanded. I'm happy to share with you some of my favorites from my youth, family, and friends from around the world, as well as some of my own unique creations.

MOM'S BROCCOLI SOUP

The winters get really crazy cold in Illinois. Soup season is a necessary thing to keep us warm from October to March. My mom used to whip up this standby favorite a few times a week when the weather was cold. I loved how satisfying, creamy, and warm it made me feel. I was also the strange kid that loved broccoli. I called them little trees when I was a toddler, apparently. Always obsessed with trees and the movement that lives in balance. Tall and sturdy, trees were and are my heroes.

I've updated her soup a bit with coconut milk to make it extra-creamy. Almond milk works well, too. I substituted nutritional yeast for her American cheese.

SERVES 4

1 white onion, chopped	1 teaspoon cayenne pepper
4 cloves garlic, chopped	1 teaspoon black pepper
1 tablespoon nondairy butter	6 shakes hot sauce
1 pound fresh broccoli	4 cups almond milk
2 carrots, chopped	½ cup nutritional yeast
4 cups vegetable broth	½ tablespoon cornstarch

Sauté the onion and garlic in the nondairy butter in a large saucepan.

Add the broccoli and carrots to the saucepan and cook for a few minutes.

Add the vegetable broth, spices, and hot sauce, and cook for a few minutes.

Stir in the almond milk and nutritional yeast slowly.

Add the cornstarch slowly and stir it constantly until the desired thickness.

Remove from the heat and serve.

ENJOY!

RED SOUP

It's silly to ignore some of the incredibly awesome benefits that some foods naturally hold for us. Beets are amazing for our blood health. Blood seems like a funny thing to keep healthy, but seeing that it pumps through our entire body and we need loads of it to survive, keeping our blood flowing happy and free is a good plan. I fly a lot, and intuitively my body craves beets when I'm in one place for a while. I imagine my body is a little compressed from so much time on long flights. Circulation can get stuck. My legs can throb sometimes after a long flight for a few days, so I'm careful to take it easy and get the vibrancy back with yoga and, of course, our friend the beet. One day, on a mission to make beet soup, I gathered every red vegetable I could find and had a party. The soup turned out so flavorful and creamy. I have a few special tricks for that, too. You'll see.

SERVES 4

½ red onion, chopped

1 tablespoon olive oil

1 red potato, peeled and chopped

3 carrots, chopped

1 beet, chopped

1 tomato, chopped

1 teaspoon chili flakes

1 teaspoon red pepper flakes

1 teaspoon paprika

1 teaspoon curry powder

1 teaspoon salt

1 tablespoon hot sauce

1½ cups coconut milk

½ cup parsley or spinach, chopped
  (optional)

Simmer the onion in a medium saucepan with the olive oil until the onions are soft.

Add the potato and simmer for 3 minutes.

Add the carrots, beet, tomato, and 6 cups water. Bring the mixture to a boil.

Add the spices and hot sauce, and simmer for 25 minutes.

Stir in the coconut milk and continue to simmer for 15 minutes.

Remove from the heat, and blend or use an immersion blender in the saucepan.

Top with the chopped parsley, if using.

ENJOY!

VERA'S BORSCHT

I have several amazing Russian women in my life. I don't know how exactly it happened, but it happened all at once, and it's been pretty awesome. It all has revolved around the Strala studio in New York City. I've learned how to knit; to grow things; to stay warm, hearty, and strong; to speak some conversational Russian; and to perform a few secret tricks that, if I tell you, I'll have to kill you. Just kidding on the last one. My friend Vera, who teaches at Strala in Los Angeles now, made her famous borscht for me when I visited. It's amazing how it made the whole house feel warm and cozy, and I loved the feeling of saving so many resources and using simple ingredients to make such a hearty meal. You can get into the real Russian spirit by adding a side of vodka to wash it down. Keeps you even warmer.

SERVES 4

1 red onion, chopped	1 pinch peppercorns
1 teaspoon olive oil	2 medium potatoes, peeled and
1 carrot, shredded	chopped
1 beet, shredded	1 cup kidney beans
Juice of ½ lemon	1 small cabbage, chopped
2 tomatoes, chopped	½ bell pepper, chopped
2 cloves garlic, minced	1 cup parsley, chopped
4 cups vegetable broth	1 bunch beet greens (optional)
2 to 3 bay leaves	1 teaspoon sour cream (optional)

Sauté the onion in the olive oil in a frying pan until golden brown.

Add the carrot and beet, and squeeze the lemon juice over the mixture.

Add the tomatoes and garlic.

Cook for a few more minutes and set the mixture aside.

Boil the vegetable broth in a medium saucepan.

Add the bay leaves and peppercorns to the saucepan.

Add the potatoes to the saucepan and cook for a few minutes.

Add the carrot-beet mixture to the saucepan and bring to a boil.

Stir in the beans, cabbage, bell pepper, and, if using, beet greens, slowly letting everything simmer for a minute between ingredients.

Cover and let it sit off the stove for a few minutes before serving.

Top with the parsley. Serve with the sour cream, if using.

ENJOY!

NEVER-GET-SICK SOUP

For the last several years, I haven't gotten sick. I've wondered occasionally why this is, but I haven't dwelled too much. I don't want to chase away my luck. I have a theory, though: when I got super-interested in regular self-care and spending my time doing what inspires me and affects positive change in the world, my body adjusted to support me. It's stronger than ever (although I'm practicing yoga less), healthier than ever (although I'm on an airplane more), and I feel fantastic from the inside out. I take good care of myself and prioritize mental and physical clarity, positive interactions, and enjoying each moment. Also, this soup helps. When I start to feel a tad bit drained, I whip up a batch, take a few deep breaths, and rest. Then I'm all set to get back to feeling energized and excited. I'm sure scientists will learn at some point that health isn't only about what you eat and what you do, but also about how you feel about life in general. More emphasis on getting excited about yourself and what you are interested in doing with your time is not only fun, but can sustain your vitality and keep you in superhero mode.

SERVES 2

4 ounces rice noodles	1 teaspoon curry powder
4 shakes hot sauce	1 teaspoon crushed red pepper flakes
1 tablespoon soy sauce	½ cup coconut milk
1 inch ginger, grated	1 tablespoon nutritional yeast

Boil 2 cups water in a medium pot.

Add the rice noodles to the pot and stir. Cook for 5 minutes.

Remove from the heat. Cover and let it set for 10 minutes.

In a separate saucepan over medium heat, boil 2 cups water.

Add the hot sauce, soy sauce, ginger, and spices to the saucepan. Mix well.

Add the rice noodles to the saucepan and combine everything well.

Add the coconut milk and simmer for 2 to 4 minutes. Remove from the heat.

Top with the nutritional yeast.

ENJOY!

EASY MISO SOUP

Japanese culture, design, and, of course, food are things that I aim to bring more of into my everyday life. Tackling miso soup at home had intimidated me for years until I actually gave it a try. Just like most other soups, it's pretty tricky to mess up and has a surprising amount of flexibility in the range of ingredients. Give it a try! As they say in Japan, *itadakimasu* (pronounced *ee-tah-dah-kee-mahs*), literally "I humbly receive," with a slight bow and hands in *namaste* for extra fun. The meaning is appreciation for where the food comes from, for the land and sun, and for the workers who bring the food to our plates. It's about honoring the connectedness of nature and the hardworking people who bring the meal to us. It's also an expression of appreciation for our lives and the people and things that sustain us: nature, sun, and air. Good stuff.

SERVES 2

1 bunch green onions, sliced	3 pieces dried kelp
2 tablespoons sesame oil	1 teaspoon red pepper flakes
1 inch fresh ginger, chopped	½ tablespoon hot sauce
1 cup dried shitake mushrooms	3 ounces soba noodles
½ cup miso	6 ounces firm tofu, chopped

Sauté the onions in the sesame oil in a large saucepan over medium-high heat.

Add the ginger, 6 cups water, mushrooms, miso, kelp, red pepper flakes, and hot sauce, and simmer for 10 to 15 minutes.

Add the soba noodles and tofu, and cook for 5 more minutes. Remove from the heat and serve.

ENJOY!

TOMATO RICE SOUP

Desperately needing to expand my repertoire of meals after having eaten out of cans and bags the first few years in New York City, I branched out and tried to re-create some familiar canned meals from the actual ingredients. It took a little longer to prepare than simply finding a can opener and warming something up, but the process was and continues to be a lot of fun. Trying new combinations, seasonings, and techniques with soups has become a favorite experiment of mine. Soups are pretty tricky to mess up, although I've had my fair share of edible disasters. The great thing about using fresh produce and spices is that you can't go too wrong. I hope you like this simple tomato rice soup that is tastier than the canned stuff by far, and pretty simple to make as well.

SERVES 2

4 tomatoes	½ cup rice
2 cloves garlic, minced	1 teaspoon tomato paste
1 red onion, chopped	1 teaspoon red pepper flakes
1 tablespoon olive oil	¼ cup coconut milk

Preheat the oven to 350 degrees Fahrenheit.

Place the tomatoes and garlic in a pan and roast for 15 to 20 minutes. Remove from the oven and allow the tomatoes to cool completely.

Sauté the onion and olive oil in a saucepan for 5 minutes, stirring occasionally.

Chop the tomatoes into eighths and add to the saucepan along with the rice, 2 cups water, tomato paste, and red pepper flakes.

Bring to a boil and simmer for 10 to 15 minutes.

Add the coconut milk and simmer for 10 minutes.

Remove from the heat and serve.

ENJOY!

CHILLY CHILI

Another favorite on the home front, my mom cooks up a hearty, warming, and flavorful chili. I like to spice it up with a little more kick than we're used to in the Midwest, so include as much heat as you like. It will warm you inside and out, either way.

SERVES 2

1 tablespoon olive oil

1 red onion, chopped

2 cloves garlic, minced

2 bell peppers, chopped

1 tablespoon brown sugar

1 tablespoon chili powder

1 teaspoon ground cumin

1 teaspoon dried oregano

1 teaspoon sea salt

1 teaspoon black pepper

1 tablespoon hot sauce

1 teaspoon red pepper flakes

1 jalapeño, chopped

4 tomatoes, chopped

1 cup black beans, cooked

1 cup kidney beans, cooked

1 cup pinto beans, cooked

Add the oil, onion, garlic, and chopped peppers to a large saucepan and warm over medium heat for about 5 minutes, stirring occasionally.

Add the remaining ingredients and bring to a boil. Reduce the heat and simmer for 30 minutes. Then remove from the heat and serve.

ENJOY!

LAZY LENTILS

The deliciousness of my mom's homemade soups was always a wonderful mystery. From the preparation of her chopping veggies and setting out spices to the first yummy scents of nourishment to come as it simmered, the soup-making process left me with the impression that it was incredibly complex. Now that my mom simply slips me recipe cards for the dishes that were such staples of my childhood, the mysteries are a little bit lifted, but the magic still remains. I see how simple and cost-effective eating well can be. It makes sense that I pretty much have re-created this cooking style on my own since my early years in New York City before returning to the original source. Thanks, Mom, for your Lazy Lentils.

SERVES 2

1 large red onion, chopped

3 carrots, cut into bite-size pieces

3 stalks celery, cut into bite-size pieces

2 tablespoons olive oil

4 cups vegetable broth

2 cups lentils, rinsed well

2 bay leaves

1 teaspoon ground coriander

1 teaspoon dried tarragon

½ teaspoon curry powder

1 teaspoon ground red pepper flakes

1 teaspoon sea salt

Sauté the onion, carrots, and celery in the olive oil in a large saucepan until the onions brown.

Add the rest of the ingredients to the saucepan. Add water if needed to cover the veggies and lentils completely.

Bring to a boil and simmer for 20 minutes.

ENJOY!

RICE NOODLE VEGGIE SOUP

I feel like I discovered the magic of rice noodles late in life, but I'm happy to be catching up now. I've been interested in Asian cultures for as long as I can remember. The normalcy of the body-mind connection, the priority on self-care, and, of course, the simplicity and nourishment of the meals make so much sense to me. While exploring noodle soup stands and all kinds of Southeast Asian fusion restaurants during my travels and in New York City, my interest has turned into an obsession. Friends I've made who live on the other side of the globe know my curiosity and interest, and take me to the insider places I would never find wandering the streets alone.

The last time I was in Malaysia, my friend Moon took me through a street market into a back alley, behind a plastic curtain, to a scene where I thought maybe I could score a mogwai to cuddle up with. We experienced a simple plate of basic rice noodles and a superdelish, spicy sauce in a dish called Chee Cheong Fun. I'm always up for anything with *Fun* in the title. I've been trying to re-create this dish ever since that day, and I think I finally got it, but I have added in some veggies to make it more of a meal than a snack.

SERVES 2

4 ounces rice noodles

1 tablespoon nondairy butter

½ red onion, chopped

2 cloves garlic, chopped

3 carrots, chopped

1 sweet potato, chopped

2 tablespoons hoisin sauce

1 tablespoon hot sauce

1 orange or red bell pepper, chopped

1 handful kale or spinach, chopped

Boil 2 cups water in a medium saucepan.

Add the rice noodles and cook for 5 minutes. Strain and set them aside.

In a medium saucepan, add the nondairy butter and onion. Sauté until the onion begins to brown.

Add the garlic to the saucepan and sauté for a few moments.

Add 4 cups water and mix well.

Add the carrots, potato, and sauces. Bring to a boil and simmer for 15 minutes.

Add the bell pepper and kale. Simmer for 20 minutes.

Add the cooked noodles and stir constantly for 1 minute.

Remove from the heat and serve.

ENJOY!

GRANDMA'S FARM VEGGIE SOUP

A visit to Grandma's house always centers around food. Whether it's time for a big dinner or relatives dropping by for a visit, there is always something to munch on within arm's reach. Once I started having friends over in my home in New York City, I realized not just the necessity of feeding people at a mealtime, but also the fun of having a nice homemade spread of goodies available all the time. Food keeps a group engaged and provides another reason—besides great company, of course—to get together. Once the food is gone, it's almost time to go. It all makes sense now why there is always so much variety of yummy dishes, sides, and desserts on Grandma's table. She wants us there, which is supersweet. We're always welcome and encouraged to stay for as long as we like. We want to be there, too. We love to visit with each other, and we love the food. Grandma's veggie soup is one of my favorite staples. I'll have a big bowl of it for lunch, supper, or as a late-night snack. It hits the spot and powers me up anytime of day.

SERVES 2

4 cups vegetable broth

8 ounces pasta noodles

1 tablespoon nondairy butter

½ red onion, chopped

4 carrots, chopped

2 stalks celery, chopped

2 tomatoes, chopped

2 bouillon cubes

Salt and pepper, to taste

Boil the vegetable broth in a medium saucepan. Add the pasta noodles and cook for 15 minutes.

Heat the nondairy butter and onion in a skillet. Sauté until the onions are soft.

Add the carrots, celery, tomatoes, salt, and pepper to the skillet. Cook for 5 minutes, stirring constantly.

Combine the cooked pasta, veggie broth, onion, carrots, celery, and tomatoes. Add the bouillon cubes.

Simmer for 15 minutes.

Remove from the heat and serve.

ENJOY!

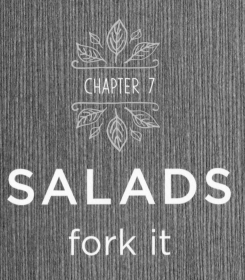

CHAPTER 7

SALADS
fork it

Big salads with fresh and savory dressings come to mind when I daydream about my ideal lunch. In my hometown in Illinois, Grandma will make the biggest spread for lunch, because my uncles, many of whom are farmers, wake up before the crack of dawn and take a lunch break when the sun is at its highest and hottest, and they are at their hungriest. At Grandma's house, they are greeted with a giant spread: everything from bread, ham roast, fruit salad, and lots of veggies. The salads are the real standout here. Carrot salads, mixed salads, warm salads, cold salads, noodle salads, Jell-O salads, green salads, and bean salads! Every dish, pot, and pan in the house is filled to the brim and spread on the table without an inch of space uncovered. We are grateful for the feast.

I have kept this spirit alive since moving to New York City. I've tried to adjust the meals to a more city vibe: hummus salads, thinly chopped veggie salads with light olive oil dressings, and fruit salads spread across my kitchen table in my downtown loft. Where my family is from, eating the biggest meal around noon makes perfect sense given their schedule, workload, and environment. Enjoying a nice, big, substantial meal in the middle of the day makes a lot of sense to me as well, even in the city. I like to eat this way when I have time, or rather *make* time in my schedule.

Whether you're preparing for a family of dusty farmers, your family/kids, friends, or yourself, I hope you are excited and fulfilled from my table to yours. The next time you have lunch, linger a little longer.

make your own rules cookbook

DEVIOUS DIJON SALAD

When I started to really get healthy with cooking, I found myself with piles of produce. This could have been an exciting opportunity, or a big bag of boring, depending on how you looked at all those veggies. Not being a fan of boring or bland, I decided to experiment with making my own dressings. The ones from the supermarket were too filled with loads of preservatives, sugars, and other junk that canceled out eating all those veggies in the first place. There had to be a better way. Devious Dijon is one of my favorite "better ways." I eat this salad many times a week in my kitchen.

SERVES 2

2 tablespoons olive oil

4 tablespoons balsamic vinegar

1 tablespoon Dijon mustard

3 shakes hot sauce

1 inch fresh ginger, sliced

Juice of ½ lemon

Juice of ½ lime

1 cup arugula

1 cup fresh spinach, lightly chopped

1 stalk celery, chopped

½ cup broccoli, chopped

½ red bell pepper, chopped

½ avocado, pitted and chopped

2 tablespoons peanuts, chopped

Combine the olive oil, balsamic vinegar, Dijon mustard, hot sauce, ginger, lemon, and lime in a small bowl, whisking until smooth to create the dressing.

Mix the arugula, spinach, celery, broccoli, and pepper in a large bowl. Add the Dijon dressing to the salad and stir until everything is evenly dispersed.

Top with the avocado and peanuts.

ENJOY!

ALMOND-CREAMED CURRY SALAD

I spent a whirlwind week in India recently: Bangalore, Mumbai, and Delhi in just a few days. I was there to train a new crop of Strala instructors, but of course I was also on a search for the meaning of life and the best way I could serve in it, as one does in India.

I hope to go to India at least once a year to visit friends I've made and enjoy the sweetness of the heart of the culture. Showing yourself and your heart through gifts of food is a special kind of nourishment I want in my life wherever in the world I go.

This Indian curry salad is infused with my favorite shortcuts and ingredients from back home, like Dijon mustard and almond butter. I think it's fair to say that I have a bit of an almond butter obsession. If almond butter is in the dish, I'm up for it. I have more than five different kinds of almond butter in my cabinet at all times. I love to experiment with making my own, and I often find myself staring at the nut-butter section of the market in wonder. I spread it on toast and fruit, bake it in cookies, use it in frosting for cakes, in sauces for main dishes, and even over pasta. I know, I get weird with almond butter, but I haven't disappointed a hungry belly yet. So don't judge this combo until you try it!

SERVES 4

3 tablespoons almond butter

1 teaspoon red pepper flakes

¼ cup almond or coconut milk

4 shakes hot sauce

½ red bell pepper, chopped

1 inch fresh ginger, sliced

½ tablespoon Dijon mustard

1 cup kale, chopped

⅛ cup cranberries

2 carrots, shredded

2 stalks celery, chopped

½ cup green beans, chopped

Blend almond butter, red pepper flakes, coconut milk, hot sauce, red bell pepper, sliced ginger, and Dijon mustard in a high-powered blender until smooth to create the dressing.

Mix the kale, cranberries, carrots, celery, and green beans in a large bowl.

Add the almond dressing to the salad, and stir until everything is evenly distributed.

ENJOY!

CHILL RANCH SALAD

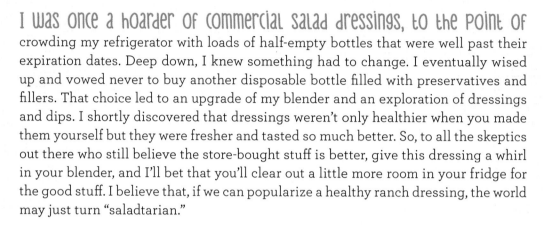

I was once a hoarder of commercial salad dressings, to the point of crowding my refrigerator with loads of half-empty bottles that were well past their expiration dates. Deep down, I knew something had to change. I eventually wised up and vowed never to buy another disposable bottle filled with preservatives and fillers. That choice led to an upgrade of my blender and an exploration of dressings and dips. I shortly discovered that dressings weren't only healthier when you made them yourself but they were fresher and tasted so much better. So, to all the skeptics out there who still believe the store-bought stuff is better, give this dressing a whirl in your blender, and I'll bet that you'll clear out a little more room in your fridge for the good stuff. I believe that, if we can popularize a healthy ranch dressing, the world may just turn "saladtarian."

SERVES 4

1 cup cashews

¼ cup almond or coconut milk

1 tablespoon maple syrup

Juice of ½ lemon

Juice of ½ lime

¼ red onion, sliced

1 clove garlic

1 to 3 parsley sprigs

1 teaspoon dill

¼ teaspoon sea salt

¼ teaspoon black pepper

1 cup of romaine lettuce, chopped

4 radishes, sliced

¼ cucumber, sliced

1 stalk celery, chopped

1 carrot, chopped

½ red bell pepper, chopped

Blend the cashews, almond milk, maple syrup, lemon and lime juices, onion, garlic, parsley, dill, salt, and pepper to create the dressing.

Mix the romaine, radishes, cucumber, celery, carrot, and bell pepper in a large bowl.

Add the dressing to the salad, and stir until everything is evenly distributed.

ENJOY!

MALAYSIAN MANGO MASH-UP

A favorite of my Malaysian friend Erna Malia, and now a favorite of mine in New York City, this mango mixture is incredibly satisfying and full of rich flavor. It's deceptively easy, making it an impressive meal for guests, and it comes with the exotic and tantalizing culture of Southeast Asia.

SERVES 2

1 small green mango, chopped

5 shallots, chopped

¼ cup chopped bird's-eye chilies

½ cucumber, sliced

Juice of 1 lime

2 tablespoons brown sugar

1 tablespoon sesame oil

1 tablespoon soy sauce

2 tablespoons peanuts, chopped

1 pinch black pepper

Combine all the ingredients in a large bowl, and stir until everything is evenly distributed.

ENJOY!

KALIEN INVASION

Kale has invaded the brains of the health conscious. There is no doubting the superpower of the big K. The only thing holding us back is how daunting a big piece of kale can seem. A kale leaf is massive and looks more like a houseplant than a salad ingredient. However, once you get in there and learn the magic of massaging your kale, those babies tame right down and are ready to jump in your bloodstream and get you supercharged from the inside out. If you haven't had the pleasure of giving kale a full rubdown yet, fair warning: this intimate culinary act will have you remembering your first time forever.

SERVES 2

3 stalks kale, broken up into manageable pieces

½ lemon

2 stalks celery

¼ orange bell pepper, chopped

¼ green bell pepper, chopped

¼ yellow bell pepper, chopped

⅛ cup raisins

½ avocado, pitted and chopped

Place the kale in a large bowl and squeeze the lemon juice over it.

Massage the kale–lemon juice combination until it shrinks up a bit, about 2 minutes.

Mix in the celery, peppers, raisins, and avocado.

ENJOY!

THAI PAPAYA SALAD

Here is another dish inspired by Southeast Asia and my friend Erna, who I met at a yoga class I led in Kuala Lumpur on a helicopter pad. As I travel more and more, I become increasingly fascinated by the variety and uniqueness of spices in each location and culture. One of my favorite explorations is the range of flavors, spices, and zests that Southeast Asian cultures bring to their fruits and veggies. This Thai Papaya Salad is one of my favorite treats.

SERVES 2

1 to 2 bird's-eye chilies

2 cloves garlic

2 cups shredded green papaya

2 tablespoons toasted peanuts, chopped

1 to 2 stalks long beans, cut into different lengths

Juice of ½ lime

1 tablespoon soy sauce

Brown sugar, to taste

Pound the chilies together with the garlic using a mallet.

Combine the remaining ingredients and mix well.

ENJOY!

CARUGULA SALAD

Creating made-up names of dishes is good, clean fun. *Carugula* is a mashed-up name I came up with to describe cranberry, arugula, and walnuts as the main standouts in this salad. It's my healthy response to the Waldorf salad, which is typically drowned in mayo. My simplified version is superdelish and will leave you feeling revitalized.

SERVES 2

2 tablespoons balsamic vinegar

1 tablespoon olive oil

2 shakes hot sauce

½ tablespoon nutritional yeast

1 teaspoon red pepper flakes

1 pinch sea salt

½ teaspoon black pepper

½ cup cranberries

4 cups arugula

½ cup walnuts

Combine the balsamic vinegar, olive oil, hot sauce, nutritional yeast, red pepper flakes, salt, and pepper in a small bowl, whisking until smooth to create the dressing.

Mix the cranberries, arugula, and walnuts. Add the dressing to the salad and stir until everything is evenly dispersed.

ENJOY!

VIEQUES SALAD

I have the rough job of spending time in some of the world's most beautiful places, learning from amazing chefs about local and global cuisine. While at the W Hotel in Vieques putting together the Strala program, as well as some healthy choices on the hotel's menu, I learned a bit about Puerto Rican cooking: superdelicious, but a bit heavy for my everyday needs. After messing around in the kitchen for a while, Chef Fernando and I came up with a collaboration salad. New York City meets Vieques: creamy, crunchy, and nourishing. It will leave you feeling fantastic. And you can make it in a New York minute!

SERVES 2

4 cups spinach

1 red bell pepper, chopped

1 avocado, pitted and chopped

1 cup plantain chips

3 tablespoons balsamic vinegar

4 shakes hot sauce

1 tablespoon Dijon mustard

Combine all the ingredients in a large bowl.

ENJOY!

CANDIED ALMOND POPEYE

I've been obsessed with spinach for as long as I can remember. It has always made me feel fantastic and I have always liked the taste. I know that I was a very strange kid. I also had this desire to be strong, so I always tried to do things to build strength. Eating like Popeye was on my list of things to do daily. Relish this decadent, sweet salad treat.

SERVES 2

1 tablespoon coconut oil

1 tablespoon maple syrup

1 cup almonds

1 pinch sea salt

4 cups spinach

1 avocado, pitted and chopped

3 or 4 cherry tomatoes, halved

1 tablespoon balsamic vinegar

1 tablespoon olive oil

3 shakes hot sauce

1 tablespoon nutritional yeast

Preheat the oven to 350 degrees Fahrenheit.

Mix the coconut oil and maple syrup.

Coat the almonds in the coconut–maple syrup mixture and pat the extra moisture away.

Place the almonds on a baking sheet and sprinkle them with the sea salt. Bake for 10 to 15 minutes until toasted.

Mix the spinach, avocado, tomatoes, and baked almonds in a large bowl.

Combine the balsamic vinegar, olive oil, and hot sauce in a small bowl, whisking until smooth to create the dressing.

Add the dressing to the salad and stir until everything is evenly dispersed.

Top with the nutritional yeast.

ENJOY!

SPICY SUMMER FRESH

The summer in New York City is one of my favorite times. People are happy, relaxed, and always making weekend beach plans. Summer Fridays are in full effect, and people are outside enjoying the weather and street fairs. I love to hang out on my balcony (aka fire escape) and delight in my favorite summer salads while watching people on the streets below. This particular salad came about after I purchased a supersharp, fancy-schmancy knife. Slicing and dicing my veggies like a pro completely changed the salad experience for me. This salad is superb on its own, and is pretty darn tasty in a sandwich.

SERVES 2

1 tomato, chopped

4 olives

2 tablespoons almond milk

1 tablespoon coconut oil

1 tablespoon hummus

1 teaspoon olive oil

1 teaspoon Dijon mustard

4 radishes, sliced

1 handful spinach, chopped

½ cucumber, chopped

½ hot pepper, chopped

1 pita, toasted and chopped

1 handful watermelon, chopped

Blend half of the tomato and all of the olives, almond milk, coconut oil, hummus, olive oil, and Dijon mustard to create the dressing.

Mix the radishes, remaining tomato, spinach, cucumber, hot pepper, pita, and watermelon in a large bowl.

Add the dressing to the salad and stir until everything is evenly dispersed.

ENJOY!

CHAPTER 8

SANDWICHES & WRAPS

grab it

Sandwiches and wraps can be the perfect solutions when hunger strikes midday. They are fast to put together and easy to gobble down, and although they have a fairly bad reputation for being unhealthy, they are actually supersimple to make nourishing and delicious. A lot of the wraps that I have discovered while creating in my kitchen have come out of leftover greens and veggie combos and the desire for a little more substance (and portability) than a big salad could give me.

Let's give our friends the sandwich and the wrap a fresh reputation by moving on from big plastic-bin days of mystery with smooshed-together contents and popularizing their amazing potential for radiance. **ENJOY!**

CREAMY SPINACH-RADISH SANDWICH

I remember the day I decided I needed to buy a supersharp knife for my kitchen. I was really getting into cooking and chopping veggies, and wondering how creative I could get if I could slice veggies superthin, gourmet-style. I hopped on over to a local shop and discovered a small area in the back, where a knife ninja was giving carrot-slicing demos. I shared with him my strong desire to immediately own a sharp knife. I knew I was in the right place when he smiled back at me like I was a little crazy but in a fun way. From that day forward, I have been hooked.

A lot of salad and wrap discovery came out of the ability to thinly slice things to wrap up. Carrots and radishes were the first on my list. This creamy radish delight was born of carefully putting my new sharp knife to work.

SERVES 1

3 tablespoons hummus

½ inch fresh ginger, chopped

½ teaspoon curry powder

Juice of ½ lemon

1 tablespoon olive oil

1 tablespoon coconut oil

3 shakes hot sauce

½ tablespoon Dijon mustard

1 tablespoon nutritional yeast

1 handful spinach, chopped

1 cremini mushroom, sliced

1 carrot, sliced

1 radish, sliced

2 slices sprouted-grain bread

Combine the hummus, ginger, curry powder, lemon, oils, hot sauce, Dijon mustard, and nutritional yeast in a small bowl, whisking until smooth to create the dressing.

Mix the spinach, mushroom, carrot, and radish in a large bowl.

Add the hummus dressing to the vegetables, and stir until everything is evenly distributed.

Apply the mixture in an even layer across a slice of bread.

ENJOY!

NOT-MUSHY VEGGIE BURGER

There are far fewer things worse in the land of veggie burgers than a mushy burger. On a constant quest to find new places to try different veggie-burger combos, the winner is substantial, pretty solid in consistency, and a little crispy on the outside. This DIY version is supersimple to make at home and comes out the right way every time.

SERVES 2

2 cups black beans

1 cup cooked lentils

1 cup breadcrumbs

1 egg replacer

5 shakes hot sauce

1 tablespoon nutritional yeast

1 teaspoon turmeric

1 teaspoon red pepper flakes

1 tablespoon olive oil

1 teaspoon sea salt

1 teaspoon black pepper

2 buns

2 pieces iceberg lettuce (optional)

½ tomato, sliced (optional)

2 tablespoons ketchup (optional)

2 tablespoons Dijon mustard (optional)

½ cup bread-and-butter pickles (optional)

Preheat the oven to 350 degrees Fahrenheit.

Mash the beans and lentils with a fork in a large bowl.

Add the breadcrumbs, egg replacer, hot sauce, nutritional yeast, and spices (except for the salt and pepper) slowly. Mix well. Refrigerate for 10 minutes. Remove after chilled and form two 6-ounce patties.

Place the patties on a baking sheet with olive oil, and season with the salt and black pepper.

Bake the patties for 20 minutes, flipping halfway through.

Serve on the buns and top with the lettuce, tomato, ketchup, Dijon mustard, and pickles, if desired.

ENJOY!

MUSHROOM TACOS

Tacos are a superbig favorite of mine. It probably has something to do with living in downtown New York City and being close to so many amazing taco stands. During the summer, I replace going for coffee or tea with taco dates. I'm obsessed with loads of the spicy sauces that different places use. There is one truck that I frequent that named its famous sauce "crack sauce," which I'm sure is a decadent combination of Thousand Island dressing, hot sauce, and some secret tricks. Tacos have that range and ability to hold humor in a seriously satisfying meal. I hope you like one of my favorite versions of the mushroom taco I make at home on the regular.

SERVES 2

1 tomato

4 shakes hot sauce

1 teaspoon red pepper flakes

1 tablespoon Dijon mustard

1 teaspoon nutritional yeast

1 tablespoon vegan mayonnaise

¼ red onion, diced

1 tablespoon nondairy butter

¼ cup diced celery

¼ cup diced cilantro

1 handful shitake mushrooms, chopped

2 tablespoons cooked rice

2 tablespoons cooked black beans

2 corn tortillas

Blend the tomato, hot sauce, red pepper flakes, Dijon mustard, nutritional yeast, and vegan mayonnaise until smooth. Set aside.

Sauté the onion in nondairy butter in a medium saucepan over medium heat until the onion is softened and brown.

Add the celery and cilantro, and stir to combine.

Add the mushrooms, rice, and beans, stirring constantly.

Add ½ of the tomato mixture to the saucepan, and stir until well combined and warm.

Warm the tortillas in a skillet for 30 seconds.

Wrap the mushroom mixture in the tortillas.

Top the tacos with the remaining tomato mixture.

ENJOY!

PARADISE ISLAND TOAST

I'M LUCKY to be able to travel so much. I've always wanted to have friends around the world, and I love the idea of universal connection. I've found in my travels that there are very few differences among most people, and it's heartwarming to see the universal ideas of love and connection expressed diversely through culture. Expressing yourself through food is an adventure that is pretty easy to work into your home kitchen. When I'm city-bound for what feels like too long, and I get that island itch, instead of being bummed, I make myself some Paradise Island Toast and bring the magic and color of island life into my urban day.

SERVES 1

2 tablespoons hummus

1 tomato

3 shakes hot sauce

½ cup almond or coconut milk

Juice of ½ lemon

2 cups spinach, chopped

2 slices bread

Blend the hummus, tomato, hot sauce, almond milk, and lemon juice until smooth to create the dressing.

Mix the spinach with the dressing.

Toast the bread and spread the mixture on it to make your sandwich.

ENJOY!

TOFU TOWER TOAST

NYC is filled with so many great restaurants representing any cuisine of your interest. Being on a health quest for so many years now, I'm always searching for great fresh food options that have flavor. I find myself creating my own meals at nice restaurants by ordering several sides and piling them all together in one entree of sorts.

The idea for Tofu Tower Toast came out of a brunch excursion ordering veggies, tofu, and toast, and stealing garnishes from friends' plates. I was so happy with my creation that I started to re-create it at home.

SERVES 1

1 tablespoon soy sauce

1 tablespoon maple syrup

1 teaspoon crushed red pepper
   flakes

1 teaspoon crushed black pepper

3 slices tofu, drained and patted dry

2 slices sourdough bread

2 leafs lettuce

6 bread-and-butter pickles

½ tomato, sliced

1 tablespoon Dijon mustard

Preheat the broiler with a rack 6 inches from the heat.

Combine the soy sauce, maple syrup, and spices in a baking dish.

Transfer the tofu slices to the baking dish and mix well until the tofu is coated.

Broil the tofu for 5 minutes on each side for a total of 10 minutes.

Toast the sourdough bread in the broiler for a couple of minutes.

Assemble the sandwich with the bread, tofu, lettuce, pickles, tomato, and Dijon mustard.

Drizzle the soy-sauce marinade on the pile and top with the second slice of bread.

ENJOY!

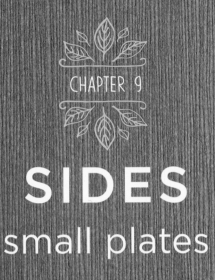

CHAPTER 9

SIDES
small plates

SIDES ARE REALLY LIKE SMALL PORTIONS OF AWESOMENESS that can be easily paired up with a few other friends for an amazing meal. It's unfair to scoot these beauties to the edges of the plate when they are always front and center ready. We all have our favorites that we can combine to become a whole meal easily. Since my first exposure to a buffet at a family reunion when I was barely big enough to hold my own plate and serve myself, I've been a big fan of combining mashed potatoes, spinach, and baked beans for a whole meal. Sides always looked the most appealing to me, and so fun to fill my plate with, especially with those handy paper plates with the little sections for everything. I encourage you to not underestimate the power of the side dish. You may discover a few new favorites you'll want to make a big batch of for the week and pair up to complete your balanced meal.

RAINBOW CEVICHE

This rainbow ceviche is inspired by Chef Javier from the W Hotel in Vieques, Puerto Rico. I was leading a retreat, which also included a healthy cooking class, and we learned how to make Chef Javier's rainbow ceviche, which had been inspired by *Make Your Own Rules Diet* and merged with the Vieques lifestyle and his global experiences. Javier, originally from Puerto Rico, has spent many years in New York City training in Japanese cuisine by working as a chef at Nobu. This explains his love of fusing color and spices and his attention to design and detail. I'm so drawn to his W Vieques creations!

SERVES 2

Juice of 1 lime

Juice of 1 lemon

¼ cup olive oil

1 teaspoon of shichimi togarashi spice

½ aji amarillo (Peruvian yellow chili pepper), or 1 teaspoon of aji amarillo powder

1 cup chickpeas, chopped

1 cup broccoli, chopped

1 red or orange pepper, chopped

3 radishes, chopped

¼ cucumber, chopped

2 carrots, chopped

Blend the lime and lemon juices, olive oil, shichimi togarashi, and aji amarillo until smooth.

Mix the chickpeas and vegetables with the blended sauce in a large bowl.

Chill in the fridge for at least 1 hour.

ENJOY!

GARLIC MASH

At family reunions, I was the kid who loaded up my plate with sides and skipped the main event. I loved the buffet style because a wide variety of choice was in play for mealtime. This was awesome as a kid. Usually your food was placed in front of you and you ate what was on it. At the buffet, *I* was in charge. My top choices were always mashed potatoes, baked beans, and spinach.

I suppose that I'm a sides gal at heart. This garlic mash is an updated version of what I piled on my plate at family reunions. Midwestern cooks aren't known for their use of garlic and spices so much; we keep it supersimple and all about the natural taste of the food. Living in the big city and traveling, I've grown to love all sorts of flavor and spice. Savor this simple-to-make, superyummy garlic mash.

SERVES 1

4 potatoes, chopped

4 cloves garlic, chopped

½ cup almond milk

2 tablespoons nondairy butter

1 tablespoon maple syrup

4 shakes hot sauce

1 tablespoon crushed red pepper flakes

1 teaspoon curry powder

1 teaspoon crushed black pepper

1 pinch sea salt

Preheat the oven to 350 degrees Fahrenheit.

Boil the potatoes in a large pot of water for 10 minutes or until tender. Drain and set aside.

Roast the garlic on a cookie sheet for 10 minutes or until brown.

Mash the potatoes in a large bowl.

Add the almond milk, nondairy butter, maple syrup, hot sauce, spices, and roasted garlic. Mix well.

Serve immediately.

ENJOY!

SPINACH RICE AND BEANS

This side for sure can be a stand-alone meal. I've enjoyed this many times on at-home workdays and at-home goof-off days. It's always supersatisfying and delish.

SERVES 1

3 cloves garlic

1 tablespoon olive oil

4 cups fresh spinach

1 cup cooked rice

1 cup cooked black beans

4 shakes hot sauce

1 teaspoon curry powder

1 teaspoon red pepper flakes

1 teaspoon black pepper

1 pinch sea salt

Sauté the garlic in the olive oil in a medium saucepan.

Add the spinach and stir constantly until it wilts.

Add the rice, beans, hot sauce, and spices, and stir constantly until combined well and warmed.

ENJOY!

GRILLED COCONUT CORN

When I was growing up in Illinois, there were entire festivals dedicated to corn. There is a parade with a queen chosen, bands on every corner, kids dressed up as scarecrows, and lots of corn on the cob. Most of the corn grown in Illinois is not for consumption. Fun fact: my family's farm sells their corn to be used for plastics in the windshields of cars. The corn on the cob for the festival comes mostly from local gardens and the grocery store. As an adult, I can barely resist corn on the cob when I see it at a buffet or on a menu. You can take the girl away from the farm, but you can't take the corn on the cob away from the girl. Relish this coconut version I like to make in the fall and dazzle my city friends with as we hang around my kitchen table and I share stories of Midwestern cornfield days.

SERVES 2

1 cup fresh coconut, chopped

½ cup nondairy butter

1 tablespoon black pepper

1 tablespoon crushed red pepper flakes

1 pinch sea salt

2 stalks corn

Preheat the broiler with a rack 6 inches from the heat.

Blend the coconut, nondairy butter, and seasonings until smooth.

Coat the corn with half the coconut-butter blend.

Place the corn in a baking dish and broil for 10 minutes or until browned.

Flip the corn and broil the other side for an additional 10 minutes or until browned.

Remove from the heat and add the remaining coconut-butter blend to the corn.

ENJOY!

GARLIC FRIES

Fries are so yummy that they really shouldn't be forbidden. I'll admit that I'm that girl who orders a salad and a side of fries whenever I have the chance to *share* with someone else (please don't tell me I'm the only one).

We didn't have fries very often when I was growing up, so they were a super-rare treat. Now that I'm a grown-up, I can eat whatever I want. The reality, of course, is, while we can eat whatever we want, we also have to deal with what that does to us. My homemade garlic fries are such a delicious, guilt-free treat: light, crispy, and oh so satisfying. The best of both worlds.

SERVES 4

2 tablespoons nondairy butter

½ tablespoon maple syrup

2 heads garlic, chopped

½ tablespoon sea salt

½ tablespoon black pepper

4 potatoes, thinly sliced lengthwise

Preheat the oven to 350 degrees Fahrenheit.

Melt the butter, and combine with the maple syrup, garlic, salt, and pepper in a medium bowl.

Dip the potato slices in the butter mixture and dab the excess with a paper towel.

Bake the potatoes on a baking sheet for 20 minutes.

Flip the potatoes and bake for another 10 to 15 minutes or until crisp.

Remove from the heat and drizzle the remaining butter mixture on top.

ENJOY!

VEGGIE PASTA SALAD

Pasta salad is another Midwest-nostalgia side dish that is fun to enjoy as an entree or a snack. I love playing around with different veggie, pasta, and sauce options. This is my favorite go-to combo that I've come up with so far. I love serving it up for potlucks and casual dinner parties.

SERVES 4

2 tablespoons balsamic vinegar

1 tablespoon olive oil

½ tablespoon Dijon mustard

½ tablespoon nutritional yeast

1 teaspoon turmeric

1 teaspoon red pepper flakes

1 teaspoon curry powder

4 cups cooked pasta

2 stalks celery, chopped

1 red or orange bell pepper, chopped

4 cremini mushrooms, chopped

1 potato, boiled and chopped

Combine the balsamic vinegar, olive oil, Dijon mustard, nutritional yeast, and spices in a small dish to create a dressing.

Mix the pasta and the chopped veggies in a medium bowl. Add the dressing to the pasta salad and stir until everything is evenly dispersed.

ENJOY!

GRANDMA GRAY'S POTATO SALAD

I don't know if Grandma made up this recipe, or if it was passed down from her mom, but I do know that I'm happy when it's on the table with a huge spoon. The hearty potatoes combined with creamy, tangy special sauce and just the right amount of crunch from the celery pieces are the epitome of comfort food. This is the kind of side dish you'll serve with a main course, and then you'll sneak to the fridge for as a midnight snack.

SERVES 4

4 white potatoes, chopped

1 cup vegan mayonnaise

4 tablespoons Dijon mustard

¼ cup coconut milk

½ cup fresh dill

1 teaspoon black pepper

1 teaspoon salt

¼ red onion, chopped

4 stalks celery, chopped

Boil 4 cups water in a medium saucepan. Add the potatoes, and boil for 10 to 15 minutes or until tender. Remove from the heat, strain, and set aside. Let the potatoes cool for 10 minutes.

Combine the vegan mayonnaise, Dijon mustard, coconut milk, dill, and seasonings in a large bowl. Add the potatoes, onion, and celery. Mix everything well.

Refrigerate for at least 2 hours before serving.

ENJOY!

CHAPTER 10

MAINS
perfect plates

YOU'VE MADE IT TO THE MAIN EVENT. THE CLASSIC standby dishes that you'll find in this chapter, as well as newer favorites from friends around the globe, have gotten me through many a hungry night—whether it was solo or with the hubs, a surprise guest, or a surprise *lots* of guests. At my house, we pretty much have an open-door poli-cy, which leads to a lot of hungry people wandering by at mealtimes. This is a long-standing tradition in my fami-ly; my mom, aunts, and grandmas always kept the kitchen stocked with not only fresh ingredients for making meals but also main meals that were ready to serve at a moment's notice. Delicious food for all is part of the reason people stay for a meaningful visit. They simply drop in to say hi, and then they get wooed by an amazing meal, so they hang around for some more visiting—and of course more treats.

Even though I live in New York, I have so much in common with my family in Illinois. Having guests is high priority because it creates a community that brings comforts of home to my hectic life in the big city. Being surrounded by people who I love, and who love me, makes anywhere I am feel like home.

The same is true no matter where you live. You simply have to cultivate the understanding that your home is open. To do this, you have to be prepared. When it's time to eat, be ready to feed not only yourself but any surprise guest that shows up. So get out the big serving dishes, spoons, and forks, and set the table. It's time to eat!

PALAK BANGALORE GRAVY

This recipe is from my friend Jaya from Bangalore. Jaya is full of joy and giggles. This lady will make you fall into fits of laughter that take over your whole self. She is a Strala guide and an inspiration to so many. We met in Bangalore, and I instantly felt like she was my little sister. She visited New York City for a few months to train at Strala, and spent a lot of time at the studio with a great group of people from all around the world. Now she is bringing ease, joy, and laughter to the people in her classes in India. I got my hands on some of her favorite Indian recipes to see if I could get them going in the kitchen. After making them, I can see our sister connection even more. Jaya and I share some of the same obsessions: spinach, chocolate, and spice to name a few. I hope you enjoy this dish as much as we do.

SERVES 4

½ red onion, sliced

¼ cup green bell pepper

1 teaspoon olive oil

1 teaspoon ginger paste

1 teaspoon garlic paste

½ tomato, sliced

3 coriander leaves

1 handful cashews

2 green chili peppers, chopped

2 bunches spinach, blanched

½ cup black beans

⅛ cup carrots, chopped

¼ cup peas, boiled

1½ teaspoons nondairy butter

Juice of ½ lime

Sauté the onion and bell pepper in the olive oil in a medium saucepan.

Add the ginger and garlic pastes, tomato, coriander leaves, cashews, and green chilies, and bring to a boil.

Add the spinach, beans, carrots, peas, and butter, and cook for 5 more minutes.

Top with the fresh lime juice.

ENJOY!

LAZY PAD THAI

There have been a few cuisines that I thought I needed to go out for because they were impossible to replicate at home. That was, of course, until I actually started to play around in the kitchen and see what I could come up with. I love going out for pad thai. I don't mind if it's from a fancy place or a hole in the wall. Now that I've played around with making my own sauce, I can't keep the secret from you, either. Bring the peanut sauce home.

SERVES 2

4 ounces dried wide rice noodles

2 tablespoons peanut butter

½ cup coconut milk

1 teaspoon red pepper flakes

4 shakes hot sauce

1 inch fresh ginger, peeled

2 cloves garlic

1 sprig parsley

Boil 2 cups water in a medium saucepan. Add the rice noodles and cook for 5 minutes. Strain and set aside.

Blend the peanut butter, coconut milk, red pepper flakes, hot sauce, ginger, garlic, and parsley until smooth.

Add the peanut sauce to the rice noodles, and stir until everything is evenly dispersed.

ENJOY!

CREAMED PEPPER NOODLES

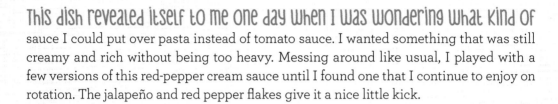

This dish revealed itself to me one day when I was wondering what kind of sauce I could put over pasta instead of tomato sauce. I wanted something that was still creamy and rich without being too heavy. Messing around like usual, I played with a few versions of this red-pepper cream sauce until I found one that I continue to enjoy on rotation. The jalapeño and red pepper flakes give it a nice little kick.

SERVES 2

4 ounces dried rice noodles or mixed vegetables

1 red bell pepper

½ cup coconut milk

1 jalapeño, chopped

1 inch fresh ginger, sliced

1 teaspoon red pepper flakes

1 teaspoon curry powder

1 teaspoon turmeric powder

1 pinch sea salt

Boil 2 cups water in a medium saucepan. Add the rice noodles and cook for 5 minutes. Strain and set aside.

Blend the red bell pepper, coconut milk, jalapeño, ginger, and spices until smooth.

Add the creamed pepper sauce to the rice noodles and stir until everything is evenly dispersed.

ENJOY!

SPICE SAUCE AND VEGGIE PLATE

The use of citrus and spice with veggies is not something I grew up with in the Midwest. We had simple, hearty, farm-inspired dishes. It wasn't until I went to Thailand that I discovered the potential of flavor combining with sweet and spice. The vibrancy of the food was completely life changing. And it was so amazing to see so many people eating piping-hot soup in the middle of summer. It was truly eye-opening. The spice combinations I sampled during the trip were incredible: everything from spicy fruits to extra-crazy spicy veggie dishes that would knock your socks off—if Thailand were cool enough for anyone to be wearing them.

SERVES 2

6 to 9 dried red chilies, deseeded and soaked in warm water for 20 minutes

3 cloves garlic

2 stalks lemongrass

1 inch fresh ginger, chopped

1 tablespoon coriander powder

2 tablespoons coconut oil

3 tablespoons peanuts, crushed

1 tablespoon tamarind juice

1 tablespoon sugar

1 tablespoon sweet soy sauce

2 cups spinach

2 stalks celery, chopped

½ cup chopped tofu

½ cup bean sprouts

½ cucumber, chopped

Blend the chilies, garlic, lemongrass, ginger, and coriander powder until smooth to create a paste.

Sauté the spice paste in the coconut oil in a medium skillet until aromatic.

Add 2 tablespoons crushed peanuts, the tamarind juice, 1 tablespoon water, the sugar, and the sweet soy sauce, and stir thoroughly. Simmer in low heat while stirring continually for about 3 minutes until the peanut sauce turns smooth.

Add the spinach, celery, and tofu to the skillet and simmer for 5 minutes until well combined and warmed.

Top with the bean sprouts, cucumber, and the remaining crushed peanuts.

ENJOY!

UDON KALE CURRY

I don't know why, but I have always felt comfortable when it comes to Japanese culture. The simple elegance and beauty in design and the philosophies based on ease of mind, calm nature, and appreciation of space have felt very natural to me. The first time I went to Tokyo, my senses were simultaneously excited and calm. Things made sense from a lifestyle perspective. The creativity and wildness of the fashion on the streets lit up my senses, and the food—the noodles, vegetables, and simple ingredients—won my heart.

SERVES 2

½ red onion, chopped

1 tablespoon olive oil

1 teaspoon curry powder

1 teaspoon red pepper flakes

½ inch fresh ginger, chopped

12 ounces udon

2 stalks kale, broken into manageable pieces

1 cup coconut milk

½ tablespoon Dijon mustard

3 shakes hot sauce

Sauté the onion in the olive oil in a medium saucepan.

Add 3 cups water, the spices, the ginger, and the udon. Bring everything to a boil, and then lower to a simmer for 10 minutes.

Add the kale, coconut milk, Dijon mustard, and hot sauce, and simmer for 5 minutes. Remove from the heat and serve.

ENJOY!

EASY PESTO AND SHELLS

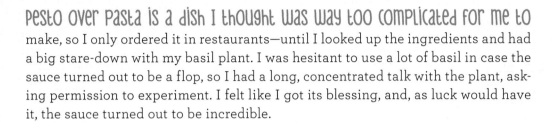

Pesto over pasta is a dish I thought was way too complicated for me to make, so I only ordered it in restaurants—until I looked up the ingredients and had a big stare-down with my basil plant. I was hesitant to use a lot of basil in case the sauce turned out to be a flop, so I had a long, concentrated talk with the plant, asking permission to experiment. I felt like I got its blessing, and, as luck would have it, the sauce turned out to be incredible.

SERVES 2

8 ounces shell pasta

½ teaspoon olive oil

1 cup fresh basil leaves

½ cup crushed pecans

1 tablespoon nutritional yeast

2 cloves garlic, chopped

½ lemon, squeezed

1 tablespoon additional olive oil

Boil 4 cups water in a medium saucepan. Add the pasta and olive oil. Cook for 10 to 15 minutes until tender. Drain and set aside.

Blend the basil, pecans, nutritional yeast, garlic, lemon, and the additional olive oil until smooth to create the pesto.

Pour the pesto over the pasta and serve.

ENJOY!

BIG BOWL OF COURAGE

When I think back to foods in my childhood that stood out to give me courage, spinach always comes to mind. I was a Popeye fan and loved that, whenever he got himself into trouble, he downed a can of spinach, powered up, and tackled whatever challenge was ahead. This is my grown-up big bowl of courage when I need to summon Popeye's strength with some extra bravery.

SERVES 2

1 cup mung beans

¼ red onion, chopped

1 tablespoon nondairy butter

2 cups fresh spinach

½ orange bell pepper, chopped

1 tablespoon cashews, chopped

2 inches ginger, chopped

1 teaspoon turmeric

4 shakes hot sauce

Juice of ½ lime

Juice of ½ lemon

Boil the mung beans in 1 cup water in a medium saucepan for 5 minutes. Drain and set aside.

Sauté the onion in the nondairy butter in a medium skillet and cook until brown.

Add the spinach, bell pepper, cashews, ginger, turmeric, and hot sauce. Stir continually and cook for 2 to 4 minutes.

Add the mung beans to the mixture, and stir until well combined. Remove from the heat.

Top with the fresh lime and lemon juices.

ENJOY!

INNER-POWER BOWL

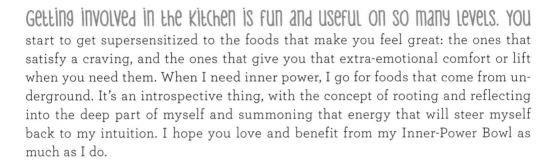

Getting involved in the kitchen is fun and useful on so many levels. You start to get supersensitized to the foods that make you feel great: the ones that satisfy a craving, and the ones that give you that extra-emotional comfort or lift when you need them. When I need inner power, I go for foods that come from underground. It's an introspective thing, with the concept of rooting and reflecting into the deep part of myself and summoning that energy that will steer myself back to my intuition. I hope you love and benefit from my Inner-Power Bowl as much as I do.

SERVES 2

½ cup rice

½ cup lentils

1 sweet potato, chopped

2 carrots, chopped

¼ beet, chopped

¼ red onion, chopped

1 tablespoon nondairy butter

1 stalk celery, chopped

1 teaspoon turmeric

1 teaspoon curry powder

½ cup coconut milk

1 tablespoon crushed peanuts

Boil 4 cups water in a medium saucepan. Add the rice and lentils together. Bring to a boil and simmer, covered, for 30 minutes or until tender. Drain and set aside.

Boil 4 cups water in a different medium saucepan. Add the sweet potato, carrots, and beet, and boil for 15 minutes or until tender. Drain and set aside.

Sauté the onion in the nondairy butter in a medium skillet until browned.

Add the celery to the skillet and mix well.

Transfer the sweet potato, carrots, beet, rice, lentils, turmeric, and curry powder to the skillet. Stir and simmer for 3 minutes.

Add the coconut milk and simmer for 3 to 5 minutes. Remove from the heat and top with the crushed peanuts.

ENJOY!

CREAMY MUSHROOM BAKE

I never really thought about what went into potatoes au gratin or why a dish of creamy baked potatoes and other veggies was called something so fancy. One evening around suppertime, however, when just a few potatoes, mushrooms, and staple ingredients were lying around the kitchen, I decided to improvise. I get it now.

SERVES 6

4 potatoes, chopped

1 cup coconut milk

¼ cup cashews

3 cloves garlic

¼ cup flour

1 tablespoon Dijon mustard

1 tablespoon nutritional yeast

1 teaspoon red pepper flakes

1 teaspoon black pepper

1 teaspoon turmeric

½ red onion, chopped

2 tablespoons nondairy butter

2 cups cremini mushrooms, chopped

6 shitake mushrooms, chopped

Juice of ½ lemon

Preheat the oven to 350 degrees Fahrenheit.

Boil the potatoes in a large pot of water until tender, about 10 to 15 minutes. Drain and set aside.

Blend the coconut milk, cashews, garlic, flour, Dijon mustard, nutritional yeast, red pepper flakes, black pepper, and turmeric to make a sauce.

Sauté the onion in the nondairy butter in a medium skillet until browned. Add the mushrooms, potatoes, and coconut sauce, and stir for 2 minutes.

Transfer to a glass baking dish and bake for 20 to 25 minutes.

Remove from the oven and top with the lemon juice.

ENJOY!

SPAGHETTI OH YES!

I ate out of a can for many meals my first couple of years in New York City. Often, it wasn't even about saving money; it was about the simplicity of preparation: open can, heat up, eat. SpaghettiOs were a trusted standby. I never felt all that amazing after downing a can, probably because the sodium intake was a week's worth. Now that I've matured (just a little), I've pledged to find a healthy version that I can feel good about. Still having fun with food keeps me inspired and fresh, like my early days in New York City when anything was possible.

SERVES 1

3 tomatoes

2 cups coconut milk

1 tablespoon tomato paste

1 teaspoon turmeric

1 teaspoon red pepper flakes

2 cloves garlic

1 tablespoon nutritional yeast

8 ounces ring-shape pasta,
   such as anelli

Blend the tomatoes, coconut milk, tomato paste, turmeric, red pepper flakes, and garlic until smooth to make a sauce.

Add the tomato sauce to a medium saucepan. Stir over medium heat until boiling.

When the sauce is boiling, add the nutritional yeast and pasta. Simmer and cook until the pasta is tender, about 20 to 25 minutes.

ENJOY!

ALMOND-CREAM CURRY

With my obsession of all things Southeast Asian, I've always been trying to cobble together something exotic and spicy with my Western staple ingredients. The first time I dared to combine almond butter and maple syrup for a savory entree instead of a smoothie, I thought I was set to make something entirely repulsive. It turned out to be one of my favorite standbys, not to mention something I could shock my friends with when they tried it for the first time. That just added to the fun.

SERVES 2

3 tablespoons almond butter

4 tablespoons coconut milk

1 tablespoon soy sauce

1 tablespoon maple syrup

1 teaspoon tomato paste

1 heirloom tomato

½ red bell pepper

½ jalapeño, sliced

1 inch fresh ginger, sliced

1 clove garlic, chopped

1 teaspoon curry powder

1 teaspoon chili powder

3 handfuls kale

8 ounces linguine

1 tablespoon olive oil

½ yellow bell pepper

Blend the almond butter, coconut milk, soy sauce, maple syrup, tomato paste, tomato, red pepper, jalapeño, ginger, garlic, and spices until smooth to make a sauce.

Steam the kale and set aside.

Boil 4 cups water in a medium saucepan. Add the linguine and olive oil. Cook for 10 to 15 minutes or until tender. Drain and set aside.

Mix the linguine, kale, and yellow bell pepper with the almond-cream sauce.

ENJOY!

TOMATO CURRY

This impressive meal is supersimple and supersatisfying. I love the mix of savory, spicy, and sweet that this dish delivers. When you've only got 10 minutes to whip up a meal, this is a solid recipe to have on hand.

SERVES 2

3 tomatoes, chopped but keeping them separate

1 teaspoon curry powder

3 tablespoons coconut milk

1 tablespoon nutritional yeast

1 teaspoon red pepper flakes

1 teaspoon black pepper

1 tablespoon honey

8 ounces rice noodles

1 tablespoon olive oil

1 tablespoon nondairy butter

Blend 1 chopped tomato, and the curry powder, coconut milk, nutritional yeast, red pepper flakes, black pepper, and honey until they make a smooth sauce. Set aside.

Boil 4 cups water in a saucepan. Add the rice noodles and olive oil to the saucepan, and cook for 5 minutes.

Remove from the heat, drain, and set aside.

Sauté the remaining chopped tomatoes in the nondairy butter in a medium skillet until softened, about 5 minutes.

Mix the noodles, tomato curry sauce, and sautéed tomatoes in a large bowl.

ENJOY!

SOHO STIR-FRY

Stir-fry is one of those meals that gets a bad rap in the health department. The oil and frying that go into fast-food mania is sometimes applied to our veggie friends. I have a simple version that is just as yummy and indulgent as the fried-up ones, but better for your energy levels, and even more flavorful. Maybe a blind taste test is due.

SERVES 2

8 ounces rice noodles

2 tablespoons olive oil

½ red onion, chopped

1 tablespoon nondairy butter

1 sweet potato, baked and chopped

1 teaspoon turmeric

1 teaspoon curry powder

1 red bell pepper, chopped

3 stalks kale, with stems removed and broken into small pieces

2 tablespoons balsamic vinegar

1 teaspoon Dijon mustard

4 shakes hot sauce

Boil 4 cups water in a saucepan. Add the rice noodles and 1 tablespoon olive oil to the saucepan, and cook for 5 minutes.

Remove from the heat, drain, and set aside.

Sauté the onion in the nondairy butter in a medium skillet until browned.

Add the potato to the skillet and stir constantly for 5 minutes.

Add the turmeric, curry powder, pepper, and kale, and stir until well combined and the kale is wilted.

Add the rice noodles to the skillet.

Combine the remaining olive oil, and the balsamic vinegar, Dijon mustard, and hot sauce in a medium bowl to create a sauce.

Add the sauce to the skillet and stir for about 1 minute until well combined.

Remove from the heat and serve.

ENJOY!

VEGGIE CASSEROLE

In the Midwest, when we all get together for meals, the table is filled with dozens of dishes. Casseroles, hot and cold salads, and soups are all piled on buffet-style. The city version looks more like one or two dishes at a time. It's more take-it-or-leave-it style rather than an endless-choices buffet. I've only now come to appreciate the variety and freedom in all those dishes set out for a meal back home. Every person at the table can eat a completely different meal, and everyone is able to have what they want. Such a nice thought. In New York City, I'd have leftovers for days if I prepared that much food, but the nostalgia of a flavorful casserole is always appealing.

SERVES 2

8 ounces penne pasta

½ red onion, chopped

1 tablespoon olive oil

4 tomatoes, chopped

1 tablespoon red pepper paste

1 cup coconut milk

5 shakes hot sauce

1 teaspoon black pepper

1 teaspoon red pepper flakes

2 cups broccoli, chopped

1 cup zucchini, chopped

2 cups cremini mushrooms, chopped

1 cup corn

1 tablespoon nutritional yeast

Juice of ½ lemon

Preheat the oven to 350 degrees Fahrenheit.

Boil 4 cups water in a medium saucepan. Add the pasta and cook for 10 to 15 minutes or until tender. Drain and set aside.

Sauté the onion in the olive oil in a medium saucepan until browned.

Add the tomatoes, red pepper paste, coconut milk, hot sauce, and seasonings to the saucepan. Stir and simmer for 20 minutes to make a sauce.

Transfer the tomato sauce and cooked pasta to a large baking dish. Add the broccoli, zucchini, mushrooms, and corn, and mix well. Sprinkle the nutritional yeast on top and bake for 20 minutes.

Remove from the heat. Top with the lemon juice and serve.

ENJOY!

make your own rules cookbook

PAD THAI TARA

I know that we've already had a killer Lazy Pad Thai (page 167) recipe, but I want to give you one that is a little more exciting in the way of feeling like a gourmet chef when you are preparing it. It's not complicated to make, but it involves using your skillet and creating a kitchen full of rich aroma that will have the neighbors banging down your door for a taste.

SERVES 2

½ cup almond butter

3 tablespoons almond milk

1 teaspoon curry powder

1 teaspoon chili powder

6 ounces rice noodles

½ red onion, chopped

4 scallions, chopped

1 tablespoon nondairy butter

2 tablespoons peanuts, chopped

1 cup bean sprouts

Mix the almond butter, almond milk, curry powder, and chili powder in a small bowl to create a sauce.

Boil 3 cups water in a medium saucepan. Add the rice noodles and cook for 5 minutes or until tender. Drain and set aside.

Sauté the onion and scallions in the nondairy butter in a medium saucepan for 5 minutes until browned.

Add the peanuts, rice noodles, and sauce to the saucepan. Stir until well combined.

Remove from the heat. Top with the bean sprouts and serve.

ENJOY!

FERNANDO'S MOFONGO

My friend Fernando, top chef at the W Hotel in Vieques, showed me how to make mofongo. He let me make one side by side with his, giving me the freedom to add what I liked as I went. Of course, it turned into a bit of a cook-off, with major props to my coach. Spices, tomatoes, and veggies, oh my! We had a great time and used all the burners. After the taste test with the kitchen staff, my version won. I think they were just being nice, although Fernando brought out and coached a hidden talent I just might have for sauces. Lobster was the main ingredient for his dish. Mine, lacking the hunk of meat, was sauced up and filled with veggies, but really, it was all about the sauce and how the plantains soaked it up. I get hungry every time I think about that cook-off now. The hardest part about being a cook is saving the dishes for your guests.

SERVES 2

½ red onion

2 cloves garlic

2 tablespoons olive oil

8 cherry tomatoes, sliced

1 teaspoon red pepper flakes

1 teaspoon black pepper

1 teaspoon salt

3 stalks asparagus

½ green bell pepper

1 cup fresh spinach

2 plantains

Sauté the onion and garlic in 1 tablespoon olive oil in a medium saucepan until browned.

Add the cherry tomatoes and 1 tablespoon water to the saucepan and simmer for 2 minutes to create a sauce.

Add the seasonings, and continue to simmer, stirring constantly. Add more water (approximately 1 tablespoon every 3 minutes) as the tomato sauce cooks down. The sauce should be thick and creamy. Set aside.

Sauté the asparagus, bell pepper, and spinach in the remaining olive oil in a medium saucepan for 5 minutes. Set aside.

Boil 2 cups water in a medium saucepan. Add the plantains and boil for 10 minutes or until tender. Remove from the heat, strain, mash, and set aside.

Transfer the plantain mash to a plate and top with the vegetables and tomato sauce.

ENJOY!

SPICY KALE AND VEGGIES

This dish is über-healthy, simple, and clean, and when you serve it to friends and family, it's also quite impressive. Spicy Kale and Veggies is the perfect answer for comfort food made healthy without any sacrifices.

SERVES 2

5 stalks kale, stems removed

Juice of 1 lemon

1 teaspoon sea salt

½ red onion, chopped

2 tablespoons nondairy butter

1 orange bell pepper

1 yellow bell pepper

2 stalks celery, chopped

1 handful cherry tomatoes, sliced

1 teaspoon curry powder

1 teaspoon red pepper flakes

Massage the kale with the lemon juice and sea salt until it shrinks, about 2 minutes.

Sauté the onion in the nondairy butter in a medium saucepan until browned.

Add the remaining ingredients to the saucepan, stirring constantly.

Remove from the heat and serve.

ENJOY!

FIVE-MINUTE VEGGIE SUSHI

DIY sushi sounded crazy to me for years. How on earth would I be qualified *to make sushi, and why would I bother, since it's so easy to get great rolls in New York City?* After visiting Tokyo a few times, I got inspired to bring more Japan into my own kitchen and decided to go for it. The great news is that it's not that complicated. There are a few tricks to getting the right amounts in the rolls. The first few times, I got a little ambitious and overstuffed, but thankfully, all the ingredients were still superyummy (if not a little messy).

SERVES 2

2 nori sheets

1 tablespoon vegan mayo or
Dijon mustard

¼ cup cooked sticky rice

2 carrots, julienned

2 cucumbers, thinly sliced

1 avocado, pitted and thinly sliced

¼ cup soy sauce

1 tablespoon wasabi

Lay out sushi mats so sticks are horizontal in front of you. Place a nori sheet on the mat, shiny side down. Add the vegan mayo to the nori sheet.

Add 2 tablespoons rice over the nori sheet. Leave a border of half an inch. Top with a little carrot and a few cucumber and avocado slices, layering in a horizontal line. Keep the layers thin.

Roll the nori sheet toward you, pressing firmly as you roll. Use the mat to squeeze your roll after it's all rolled up. Remove the roll from the sushi mat and slice the roll evenly with your knife. Repeat the process with your remaining ingredients, except soy sauce and wasabi.

Mix the soy sauce and wasabi in a small bowl for dipping.

ENJOY!

CREAMED QUINOA

Creamed quinoa came out of one of those days when there was barely anything left in my kitchen. Searching the back of the fridge and kitchen cabinets, I let my intuition take over and created this dish on the fly. Now it has transitioned to a front-and-center dish in my repertoire.

SERVES 2

2 cups quinoa

2 cups coconut milk

2 cups fresh spinach

4 shakes hot sauce

Boil 4 cups water in a medium saucepan. Add the quinoa and simmer for 5 minutes.

Add the coconut milk and spinach to the saucepan. Simmer for 5 minutes.

Add the hot sauce, and mix well. Remove from the heat and serve.

ENJOY!

GRILLED PINEAPPLE AND RICE

It dawned on me last summer, after buying a pineapple to consume pretty much every time I left my house, that I could toss that pineapple on the "barbecue" (my broiler) and wow myself with a gourmet summer snack. After a few tries at getting the perfect rub, I give you a fun summer meal you can have on the porch or, in my case, the fire escape on those long summer nights.

SERVES 2

3 large pineapple slices

2 tablespoons balsamic vinegar

1 teaspoon sea salt

1 cup cooked rice

2 tablespoons coconut milk

1 tablespoon nondairy butter

Preheat the broiler with a rack 6 inches from the heat.

Rub the pineapple slices with the balsamic vinegar and salt on both sides. Broil for about 10 minutes, flipping halfway through until both sides are browned.

Mix the rice, grilled pineapple, coconut milk, and nondairy butter in a medium skillet over high heat.

Stir and simmer for 5 minutes.

Remove from the heat and serve.

ENJOY!

CHAPTER 11

DESSERT
indulge in it

And now it's the moment we've all been waiting for—or shall I say "saving room for." Dessert is served! For me, dessert is the best part of any meal, as long as the dessert is well made. It can be a classic, comfy, cozy cookie or an interesting, unexpected flavor sensation. It doesn't matter—dessert is great. And it's one of my favorite things to serve drop-in guests whether after a meal or on its own.

So check out some of my favorites. You'll find loads from childhood that I've healthied up a bit, plus some exotic treats from friends on the other side of the globe.

What I've found from years of entertaining is that people flock to desserts, so if you have a sweet tooth or a warm heart, whip up some of these treats for yourself and your friends and keep the party going strong!

VERA'S RUSSIAN BAKED APPLES

I think I must be secretly from Eastern Europe, either in blood or spirit. I have a lot of Russians around me, mostly those I've met through Strala. We understand that life can be challenging, but we choose to work with ease. We're strongwilled, hardworking, and industrious: whether it's knitting clothing, growing food, or cooking up some delicious meals. The idea of working with what you have and creating luxury out of simplicity is something specifically wired in us. I never felt the need to spend a lot of money to live and eat well.

This baked apple recipe from my good friend Vera is insanely perfect. Not only is it one of the most delicious desserts in my repertoire, but it brings along with it a multisensory experience, filling the whole house with the feeling of warmth and comfort.

SERVES 2

1 cup walnuts

1 cup raisins

2 apples

Juice of 1 lemon

4 cinnamon sticks

2 tablespoons cinnamon

½ tablespoon honey

Preheat the oven to 350 degrees Fahrenheit.

Crush the walnuts and mix with the raisins in a small bowl to create a filling.

Remove the top and center of the apple cores, leaving the bottom of the apples intact to create a little container for the walnut-raisin filling. Make sure to leave a little of the cores at the bottom.

Pour the lemon juice into the holes. Add the walnut-raisin filling and 2 cinnamon sticks to each apple.

Place waxed paper on a baking sheet and the apples on top.

Bake the apples for about 1 hour or until fragrant. The apple skins should be wrinkled, and the juice that leaks out should be caramelized.

Remove the cinnamon sticks from the apples.

Sprinkle the powdered cinnamon and drizzle the honey on top.

ENJOY!

CHICKIE-GRANDMA'S DISH-PAN COOKIES

I called my great-grandmother Chickie-Grandma because, every time I was at her house, she was busy in the kitchen making fried chicken. She also made my favorite dessert ever: her own invention called dish-pan cookies. At her 90th birthday party held at the town hall, I remember the one moment I spent with her in a kitchen when she wasn't cooking. She told me she had lived enough life for one person and was ready to go. I remember that moment clearly and thought it was really amazing how she was so peaceful and wise to know that she was ready to move on from this life. A few weeks later, she passed away. Her spirit lives on in her dish-pan cookies. The best and most quirky thing about this recipe is that it is always different. The recipe is very forgiving with the ingredients. She used it to empty her cabinets of cereals, nuts, oats, and anything that could possibly work to fill out or add flavor to a cookie.

SERVES 8

2 cups brown sugar

2 cups sugar

2 cups olive oil

4 egg replacers

2 teaspoons baking soda

1 teaspoon salt

4 cups flour

1½ cups oats

4 cups cornflakes

½ cup chocolate chips

½ cup raisins

¼ cup coconut flakes

¼ cup walnuts

Preheat the oven to 375 degrees Fahrenheit.

Mix the sugars, olive oil, egg replacers, baking soda, and salt in a large bowl.

Add the remaining ingredients, stirring as you add each one.

Transfer to an 11 x 7-inch baking dish, and bake for 8 to 10 minutes.

Let cool for 20 minutes. Slice and serve.

ENJOY!

MOM'S "TWINKIE" CAKE

When I was growing up, we didn't keep much junk food in our house, but we did have a slightly strange quirk associated with the junk food we did have: we kept it in the dishwasher. My parents were big into the conservation of water and energy and general good-for-the-planet stuff, so we didn't actually use our dishwasher for doing dishes. We stored all the bad-for-us food in there. Gummy bears, chips, licorice, and even Twinkies. My friends always thought it was funny when I would break in to our unconventional candy drawer. What can I say, my parents were the original make-your-own-rules philosophers.

My mom also made an amazing "Twinkie" cake that she told us was healthier than eating a bunch of Twinkies. She was right. This recipe requires two days of refrigeration before eating, but it is so worth the wait.

SERVES 8

Cake

1 cup sugar

½ cup nondairy butter

2 egg replacers

2 teaspoons vanilla extract

1¾ teaspoons baking powder

1½ cups flour

½ cup almond milk

Filling

5 tablespoons flour

1 cup almond milk

1 cup sugar

½ teaspoon salt

1 teaspoon vanilla

1 cup nondairy butter

Preheat the oven to 350 degrees Fahrenheit.

To make the cake batter, mix the sugar and nondairy butter in a large bowl. Add the egg replacers and vanilla. Then add the baking powder and flour. Lastly, add the almond milk and beat until smooth.

Transfer the cake batter to two greased 9 x 9-inch cake pans. Bake for 30 to 40 minutes or until the cake sets. Leave aside.

To make the filling, mix the flour and almond milk in a small saucepan over high heat. Cook until the filling is thick, stirring continually, approximately 5 minutes. Remove from the heat and allow to cool.

Mix the sugar, salt, vanilla, and nondairy butter in a large bowl until fluffy. Add the cooled milk mixture. Beat for at least 5 minutes.

Top one cake with the filling. Place the other cake on top of the filling.

Store in the refrigerator for 2 days before eating.

ENJOY!

SPA-DIRT PUDDING

Maybe it's a Midwest thing, or maybe it's an all-over-America, childhood thing, but dirt pudding is absolute nostalgia. It's fun to bring to a summer picnic or birthday party. This cleaned-up, citified version will impress your friends. For the inner-sophisticated-philistine in all of us, have fun!

SERVES 8

Pudding

⅔ cup sugar

6 tablespoons cornstarch

¼ teaspoon salt

4 cups almond milk

2 teaspoon vanilla extract

8 ounces vegan cream cheese

1 cup of powdered sugar

Whipped Topping

14 ounces coconut milk, refrigerated overnight

3 teaspoons maple syrup

1 teaspoon vanilla extract

Dirt Topping

36 cream-filled chocolate sandwich cookies

Organic gummy worms (optional)

To make the pudding, mix the sugar, cornstarch, and salt in a large saucepan over low heat. Add the almond milk slowly, stirring continually. Cook over low heat, stirring continually for 3 minutes or until thickened.

Add the vanilla.

Cook for another 3 minutes, stirring occasionally.

Remove from the heat and let cool for 15 minutes. Pour into a large glass bowl and let set in the fridge for 3 hours.

Mix the vegan cream cheese and powdered sugar in a medium bowl, adding the powdered sugar slowly. Set aside.

Add the vegan cream cheese mixture to the pudding once the pudding is set. Mix well until combined.

To make the whipped topping, strain the coconut milk. Scoop the coconut-milk solids into a medium bowl.

Add the maple syrup and vanilla extract, and beat into a fluffy consistency.

Top the pudding with whipped topping.

To make the dirt topping, blend the cookies until their texture is crumbly.

Top the pudding and whipped topping with the dirt topping and gummy worms, if using. Serve in a small bowl (or even a flower pot).

ENJOY!

LIME CAKE

Cake is just such a simple, classic treat to serve guests and a decadent delight to have at home. To me, having a cake in arm's reach is one sign of a happy home. When I'm home from traveling for a bit, no matter how silly my schedule gets, I like to carve out the time to bake a cake. The simple pleasure of mixing, baking, waiting, and inhaling the sweet smell that fills my home helps me settle into the present moment and appreciate all that life has offered me.

SERVES 8

1 cup sugar

½ cup nondairy butter

2 egg replacers

2 teaspoons vanilla extract

1¾ teaspoons baking powder

1½ cups flour

½ cup almond milk

Juice of ½ lime

⅛ cup powdered sugar

Preheat the oven to 350 degrees Fahrenheit.

To make the cake batter, beat the sugar and butter in a medium bowl. Add the egg replacers and vanilla. Then add the baking powder and flour.

Add the milk and half the lime juice, and beat until smooth.

Transfer the cake batter to a greased 11 x 7-inch baking pan. Bake for 30 to 40 minutes or until set.

Top with the remaining lime juice and the powdered sugar.

ENJOY!

BERRY CUPCAKES

Most people know where they were during big stock market booms and busts. I remember most vividly the cupcake boom in New York City. After the massive hit of *Sex and the City*, cupcakes became all the rage. People lined up down the block to get a box for an afternoon sugar fix or a late-night snack. Not long after the success of one flower-named cupcake shop, the city flooded with new cupcake shops on practically every other corner. These shops boasted about their special trademark frostings, quirky culture, or other cupcakelike offerings. At certain places, you can even get just the frosting because, let's face it, that's what we're really after anyway.

Getting my cupcake shop on at home is a weekend pursuit all its own. I pretend I am baking for a line of hungry New Yorkers, and then invite my real hungry friends over for a treat.

SERVES 8

Cupcakes

1 cup sugar

½ cup nondairy butter

2 egg replacers

2 teaspoons vanilla extract

1¾ teaspoons baking powder

1½ cups flour

Juice of ½ lime

½ cup almond milk

1 cup strawberries, chopped

1 cup blueberries

Frosting

1 cup coconut or almond milk

¼ cup flour

½ cup nondairy shortening stick

½ cup nondairy butter

4 strawberries, chopped

1 cup sugar

1 teaspoon vanilla extract

make your own rules cookbook

Preheat the oven to 350 degrees Fahrenheit.

To make the cupcake batter, beat the sugar and butter. Add the egg replacers and vanilla. Next add the baking powder and flour. Then add the lime juice and almond milk, and beat everything until smooth.

Add half the strawberries and half the blueberries, and mix well.

Line a 12-cup cupcake baking pan with paper or foil cupcake holders.

Bake for 30 to 40 minutes or until set.

To make the frosting, combine the coconut milk and flour in a medium saucepan. Stir continually and bring to a boil. Remove from the heat and set aside to cool.

Add the nondairy shortening, nondairy butter, chopped strawberries, sugar, and vanilla to the saucepan. Beat with a hand mixer until light and fluffy. Refrigerate for at least 1 hour before applying the frosting.

Spread the frosting on top of the cupcakes.

Top with the remaining berries and serve.

ENJOY!

BIG BOWL OF AWESOME SAUCE

Sometimes you want, like, five desserts in one. This Big Bowl of Awesome Sauce makes that okay. This recipe was originally supposed to be a chocolate cake, but I added too much dark chocolate, and it didn't come out of the pan in one piece. It's too sad to throw out a cake, and it actually tasted really good. So I whipped up some pudding, organized everything in cute jars, and served them to friends. I came off looking like I had had a superchic and gourmet moment with this one. Failures sometimes lead to the greatest success, even in the kitchen.

SERVES 6

Pudding

⅔ cup sugar

6 tablespoons cornstarch

⅛ teaspoon salt

4 cups almond milk

2 teaspoon vanilla extract

Cake

1 cup sugar

½ cup nondairy butter

2 egg replacers

2 teaspoons vanilla extract

1¾ teaspoons baking powder

1½ cups flour

½ cup almond milk

2 cups dark chocolate, chopped

1 tablespoon cocoa powder or
    powdered sugar (optional)

To make the pudding, mix the sugar, cornstarch, and salt in a large saucepan over low heat. Add the almond milk slowly, stirring continually.

Cook over the low heat, stirring continually until thickened, about 3 minutes.

Add the vanilla.

Cook for another 3 minutes, stirring occasionally.

Remove from the heat and let cool for 15 minutes. Transfer to a glass bowl and refrigerate for 3 hours.

To make the cake, preheat the oven to 350 degrees Fahrenheit.

Beat the sugar and butter in a medium bowl. Add the egg replacers and vanilla. Next add the baking powder and flour. Then add the almond milk, and beat everything until smooth. Lastly, add the dark chocolate, and mix well.

Pour cake batter into six cupcake holders.

Bake for 15 to 20 minutes or until set. Allow to cool for at least 20 minutes.

Remove cupcake from holders, slice in half, and place bottoms in six glass jars or bowls. Top the cake with half the pudding, and then alternate with the cake and pudding until you reach the tops of your jars or bowls.

Sprinkle with the cocoa powder, if using. Serve.

ENJOY!

BANGIN' BROWNIES

My mom is always on a quest for healthy dessert options. I suppose this runs in the family. We often swap recipes and try to improve each other's creations. During a recent visit back home, I sampled some of her brownies. Noticing that I liked them, she handed me this recipe. I would never have guessed some of the secret ingredients that make these brownies healthier than your average gooey batch. So good and so clever. Thanks, Mom!

SERVES 8

6 tablespoons nondairy butter

½ cup flour

¼ teaspoon sea salt

½ teaspoon baking powder

1 egg replacer

1 cup sugar

1 teaspoon cinnamon

½ teaspoon cardamom

1 cup dark chocolate chips

1 teaspoon vanilla extract

½ cup cocoa powder

1 cup coconut or other nondairy
   yogurt

⅛ cup powdered sugar

¼ cup walnuts, chopped (optional)

Preheat the oven to 350 degrees Fahrenheit.

Grease an 11 x 7-inch baking dish with the nondairy butter.

Combine the flour, salt, and baking powder in a bowl and set aside.

Combine the egg replacer, sugar, cinnamon, and cardamom and set aside.

Add the butter and ½ cup chocolate chips to a medium saucepan over low heat. Cook until melted. Remove from the heat, and add the vanilla, cocoa powder, coconut yogurt, and the remaining chocolate chips.

Add the flour and egg mixtures and the walnuts, if using, and stir well.

Transfer the mixture to the baking dish and bake until a knife inserted into the cake comes out clean, about 25 minutes.

Allow it to cool in the dish for 20 minutes or until cool to the touch.

Top with the powdered sugar. Cut into squares and serve.

ENJOY!

STRAWBERRY GOOEY SHORTCAKE

Growing up, I had my fair share of strawberry shortcake dolls. The crazy thing is that, after all this time, on a recent trip home, I went into the basement to stroll through memory lane. I found all our old toys, and the dolls still smelled like strawberries! They were well preserved. I never got into the Easy-Bake Oven set as a kid, but I always craved strawberry cake after playing with my dolls. These crazy dolls inspired me after all this time to invent my own healthier version of strawberry cake.

SERVES 6

Strawberry Sauce

4 cups strawberries, chopped

¼ cup sugar

Juice of ½ lemon

Cake

1 cup sugar

½ cup nondairy butter

2 egg replacers

2 teaspoons vanilla extract

Juice of ½ lime

1¾ teaspoons baking powder

1 ½ cups flour

½ cup almond milk

1 tablespoon powdered sugar

For the sauce, combine the strawberries, sugar, lemon juice, and ¼ cup water in a medium saucepan over high heat and bring to a boil. Simmer and cook for 20 to 30 minutes, stirring occasionally. Once thickened, let set in the refrigerator for at least 30 minutes.

For the cake, preheat the oven to 350 degrees Fahrenheit.

Mix the sugar and butter in a medium bowl. Add the egg replacers, vanilla, and lime juice.

Add the baking powder and flour. Then add the milk, and beat until smooth.

Transfer a third of the cake batter to an 11 x 7-inch cake pan. Top with a third of the strawberry sauce, and repeat twice more.

Bake for 30 to 40 minutes.

Allow the cake to cool for at least 30 minutes.

Top with the strawberry sauce and powdered sugar.

ENJOY!

COCONUT CHOCOLATE MINT ICE CREAM

I grew up eating a big bowl of ice cream pretty much every night. I was super-active with sports and dance, so I'm sure this had a lot to do with the reason my body craved the extra calories. I'm convinced the ice cream tradition also led to mental satisfaction, happiness, and warm, fuzzy feelings because I never had any negative side effects from so many scoops. As an adult, I don't think my body can handle ice cream every night, but it's a treat I'm not willing to give up. It's just too yummy. I'm so ice cream obsessed that I've tried a few times to make my own. Here is a version that has actually turned out well time after time. It does take some TLC in the freezing process, but it's totally worth it.

SERVES 4

One 14-ounce can coconut milk

4 tablespoons coconut oil

3 tablespoons raw sugar

1 tablespoon cocoa powder

1 teaspoon vanilla extract

1 teaspoon peppermint extract

Combine everything in a large bowl and stir.

Freeze for 20 minutes.

Stir again. Freeze for an additional 20 minutes.

Continue to stir and freeze every 20 minutes for about an hour until you have ice cream.

Transfer to a reusable plastic container and freeze until ready to serve.

ENJOY!

ERNA'S CINNAMON NUT-BUTTER CRISPS

These crisps from my healthy friend Erna take me back to high school lunch break, cruising through the drive-through to get those crispy cinnamon churro sticks from Taco Bell. We knew they weren't healthy, but we were sugar-obsessed teens with 20 minutes of freedom a day.

When I first tried Erna's recipe, which came with a Malaysian twist because of the spring roll sheets, I was amazed at how close our cultures could be. Her recipe had an added creaminess from the nut butters. You'll love the crunchiness plus the combination of sweet and salty.

SERVES 4

1 package (25 sheets) spring roll
  sheets
½ cup coconut oil
2 tablespoons nut butter (any will do)

½ tablespoon cinnamon
1 tablespoon coconut sugar
  (or any other type of sugar)

Preheat the oven to 300 degrees Fahrenheit.

Cut the spring roll sheets into rectangular strips or use cookie cutters to make fun shapes.

Mix the coconut oil and nut butter in a large bowl.

Brush the cut sheets with the oil-butter mixture.

Mix the cinnamon and sugar in a small bowl. Sprinkle the cinnamon-sugar mixture on top of the spring roll sheets.

Place the spring roll sheets on a baking sheet, and bake in the oven for 20 minutes or until browned.

ENJOY!

GINGER COOKIES

Ginger cookies are the perfect variation of the classic sugar cookie that isn't too sweet or spicy. These cookies add just a hint of fresh ginger to make a revitalizing dessert. I borrowed from part of my classic snickerdoodle recipe, which is in *Make Your Own Rules Diet,* for the basic idea.

SERVES 8

1½ cups all-purpose flour

¼ cup cornstarch

1 teaspoon baking powder

1 4-ounce stick nondairy butter

1¼ cups sugar

¼ cup vanilla almond milk

1 teaspoon vanilla extract

3 inches fresh ginger, chopped

3 tablespoons cinnamon

Preheat the oven to 350 degrees Fahrenheit.

Mix the flour, cornstarch, and baking powder in a bowl.

Beat the nondairy butter and ⅝ cup sugar in a separate bowl until smooth.

Mix the almond milk, vanilla extract, and ginger in a separate bowl.

Add the almond milk mixture to the butter mixture, and beat everything again until smooth.

Add the dry ingredients, and beat everything once more until smooth.

Roll the dough into small balls, about 1 tablespoon each.

Mix the remaining sugar and the cinnamon in a small bowl.

Roll the dough balls in the cinnamon-sugar mixture.

Place the coated balls on a baking sheet, and bake for 15 to 20 minutes.

Remove from the oven, place on a cooking rack, and allow the cookies to cool.

ENJOY!

MOM'S OATMEAL COOKIES

One of my favorite childhood memories is coming home from school and being greeted with the comforting smell of freshly baked cookies. I remember thinking that the timing was such a weird coincidence: that they were there at the precise moment when I got home from school. My mom did a pretty good job of not spoiling us, instead making us think that the cookies weren't being made special for us. They were always for a bake sale or church dinner, but there were always a few left over.

SERVES 8

¼ cup brown sugar

1 cup sugar

½ cup nondairy butter

2 egg replacers

1 teaspoon vanilla extract

¾ cups flour

½ teaspoon baking soda

¼ teaspoon sea salt

1 teaspoon cinnamon

1 teaspoon cardamom

1½ cups oats

½ cup raisins

½ cup chocolate chips

½ cup pecans, chopped

Preheat the oven to 375 degrees Fahrenheit.

Beat the sugars and butter until smooth. Add the egg replacers and vanilla extract, and blend.

Add the flour, baking soda, salt, cinnamon, and cardamom.

Add the oats, raisins, chocolate chips, and pecans, and stir to combine.

Roll the dough into small, even balls and place on a baking sheet. Bake for 8 to 10 minutes.

Remove from the oven, transfer to a cooling rack, and let cool.

ENJOY!

SHIHO'S SHAVED ICE

Along with the art, culture, design, and noodle dishes, I have become obsessed with Tokyo's popular shaved ice. My friend Shiho, who lives there, loves to show me all her favorite places in town. We've toured many shaved-ice spots at this point, and I'm dedicated to trying as many as I can fit in my belly and schedule with every visit. It's incredibly simple and delicious—and nothing like the snow cones of my childhood. Shaved ice is a sophisticated dessert worthy of culinary praise. It's worth the long flight just to indulge. Thankfully, we can make this in the comfort of our own homes as well.

SERVES 4

4 cups ice
2 tablespoons sweetened
   condensed milk or coconut milk
4 tablespoons sweet red bean paste

Blend the ice until it's the consistency of shaved ice, about 3 minutes.

Pour the shaved ice into serving dishes.

Top with the condensed milk and red bean paste.

ENJOY!

GREEN TEA SHAVED ICE

This wide-eyed dessert will pep up your system even more than a shot of espresso. I love rotating this delicious treat into my usual routine or fascinating guests with this unexpected delight at the end of a dinner party.

SERVES 4

1 tablespoon matcha green tea powder

3 tablespoons sugar

4 cups ice

2 tablespoons condensed milk or coconut milk

4 tablespoons sweet red bean paste (optional)

Boil 1 cup water in a small saucepan.

Whisk the matcha and sugar in a small bowl.

Add ¼ cup boiling water slowly, whisking continually.

Strain and refrigerate for at least 1 hour.

Blend the ice until it's the consistency of shaved ice, about 3 minutes.

Pour the matcha-sugar mixture over the shaved ice. Add the condensed milk.

Top with the red bean paste, if using.

ENJOY!

SYRUPY BANANA

Bananas are one of my favorite fruits, probably because they are so sweet, creamy, and satisfying all at once. On their own, they are worthy enough to be a solid snack or dessert, but when used as the main ingredient in a dessert, they become super-indulgent. This recipe is simple to make and outrageously delicious. No cookies or cakes in the house? No problem. Go bananas!

SERVES 4

½ cup brown sugar

3 to 4 bananas

¼ cup coconut milk (optional)

Mix the brown sugar and 1 cup water in a medium skillet over high heat until the syrup starts to boil.

Reduce the heat to low. Add the bananas and cook until orange in color.

Place the bananas in serving dishes. Top with the coconut milk, if using.

ENJOY!

CHOCOLATE MOOSE

There is a community center in my hometown called the Moose Hall.
Lots of different groups use the space to have events. Some of the hardcore members wear baseball hats with fuzzy moose antlers on the front. It's my kind of wacky.

Chocolate mousse is fantastic for a midday snack or anytime treat. I remember those chocolate pudding packs that showed up in school lunches or at friends' houses. This version is grown up in sophistication, but I'm sure it would go over just as well with a hungry kid or member of the Moose Hall.

SERVES 2

½ cup coconut milk, refrigerated
   overnight
3 tablespoons maple syrup
1 teaspoons vanilla extract
2 avocados, pitted and chopped

2 tablespoons almond milk
1 tablespoon cocoa powder
1 tablespoon coconut sugar
1 teaspoon cinnamon

Strain the coconut milk into a small bowl. Discard the solids.

Blend the coconut milk, maple syrup, and vanilla extract until they look like whipped cream. Set aside in the fridge.

Blend the remaining ingredients, except the cinnamon. Transfer to a small serving bowl.

Serve the Chocolate Moose topped with the coconut whipped cream and cinnamon.

ENJOY!

final wishes
for you

One aspect of my life that I am so grateful for is all the travel I get to do—the places I get to experience and the people I get to meet. When I shared recipes and swapped stories with these folks, boundaries faded and cultures united. I am constantly reminded that we are more similar than we are different. We all desire to feel fantastic and radiate from the inside out. These recipes celebrate our uniqueness and strengthen our common desire to share, connect, and enjoy!

Sharing a meal is an act of kindness that begins with the heart and ends with the soul. I gain so much joy from preparing my favorite meals for others. When we give to others, we gain even greater benefits than those who are on the receiving end of our gifts. Of course we aim to please the people we feed, but we cooks are the ones left with expansive and full hearts.

I encourage you to expand your boundaries, try new things, share with new people, and let yourself be surprised by what happens next. Often it's our fear of expansion that holds us back from an unknown yet possibly amazing experience. Cooking is such an easy way to move into the unknown. Especially when you have just a little guidance. The fresh, simple, and wholesome recipes in this book will help inspire you to come up with something yummy that leaves you feeling fantastic.

Take a big, deep inhale to create loads of room inside your body and mind and a long, easy exhale to relax and revel in your creations. My wish for you is countless moments of magic making in the spirit of goofing off in the kitchen in a ridiculously happy home crowded with people you love.

ENJOY!

XO
TARA

index

Note: Page numbers in **bold** indicate recipe category lists.

acknowledgments

I owe a huge thank you to the many chefs around the world who nourish me and respond so well to my excitement for cooking. Mom, Grandma G & R, Aunt Sharon, Rindy, Mary, Shelah, and Tony back home for letting me belly up to the counter and assist in some duties.

Erna, my friend from the other side of the world who has become like a sister—making our own rules from Malaysia to Bali to NYC and beyond is the only way we roll. Leong Moon Weng, Amanda, and Lucas, thank you for taking me through the back streets of Malaysia to try authentic Chee Cheong Fun and other things I could never imagine. Henry Quek and the team, thank you for finding Miso in Jakarta because you know it's my comfort food. Shiho Ishige, thank you for our adventures in Harajuku, shaved ice, and hot noodles and springs, and lifelong friendship. Lego and Chief, for our proper Tokyo dining outings. Sandrine, for impeccable Japanese food in Paris, strong coffee with rad design, and appreciation for perfect nonchalant presentation.

Arnaud Champenois, Emily Shattan, and Sarah Doyle for all the championing and of course the delicious treat of serving my recipes at W Hotels Worldwide. Chef Fernando Coppola, thank you for the laughs from Vieques to Chicago, for the mofongo and the inspiration. Javier Melendez, thank you for kindly collaborating and the Asian-Puerto Rican integrations. To all the participants of events and classes and lectures around the world, who bring me food, thank you. I enjoy every bite and am grateful to be fed with love.

Patty Gift, thank you for letting me do this book. Reid Tracy, thank you for your guidance and support. Laura Gray, thank you for your patience, your loads of work, gobs of laughs, and your ability to elevate ideas. Sally Mason, thank you for your support and help. Charles McStravick, your designs are so fun and awesome, and I'm grateful for this book, as well as *Make Your Own Rules Diet*—they look so great because of you. Richelle Zizian, thank you for spreading the word and for the support on many levels. Erin Duprée, thank you for caring and sharing.

Andrew Scrivani, you're stuck with me now. A hearty eye and a breezy kitchen makes pretty awesome photos with your talent. Thank you. Thank you Brian Davis at Apple for the continued support. Thank you to the Strala global community for spreading the mission of empowering others to make your own rules and enjoy radiance from the inside out. You are the wellness warriors this world thrives on.

about the author

Tara Stiles is the founder and owner of Strala, the movement system that ignites freedom. Thousands of guides are leading Strala classes around the globe in partner studios, gyms, and clubs. Tara partners with Sports Club/LA and CMG, making Strala classes the first branded yoga program to be available at major gym chains.

Tara partners with W Hotels on FIT with Tara Stiles—a global program bringing Strala Yoga classes and healthy recipes to W properties around the globe. She is a collaborator with Reebok, working closely with the design team on their Reebok Yoga lifestyle range, and has authored several top-selling books, including *Slim Calm Sexy Yoga, Yoga Cures,* and, most recently, *Make Your Own Rules Diet,* which have all been translated and published in several languages. She has been profiled by *The New York Times, The Times of India,* and *The Times (UK),* and featured in most major national and international magazines. Tara is a sought-after speaker, primarily on topics of business building and health and wellness. She has lectured to sold-out audiences and internal conferences around the world, including Fortune's Most Powerful Women's Conference and events with Epsilon, Happinez, and Hay House.

Tara supports the Alliance for a Healthier Generation, President Clinton's initiative to combat childhood obesity, bringing Strala classes to 20,000-plus participating schools. Strala's flagship studio is in downtown New York City.

Visit www.tarastiles.com.

HAY HOUSE
TITLES
OF RELATED
INTEREST

YOU CAN HEAL YOUR LIFE, the movie, starring Louise Hay & Friends
(available as a 1-DVD program and an expanded 2-DVD set)
Watch the trailer at: www.LouiseHayMovie.com

THE SHIFT, the movie, starring Dr. Wayne W. Dyer
(available as a 1-DVD program and an expanded 2-DVD set)
Watch the trailer at: www.DyerMovie.com

CRAZY SEXY JUICE:
100+ Simple Juice, Smoothie, and Nut Milk Recipes to Supercharge Your Life,
by Kris Carr

CULTURED FOOD FOR HEALTH:
A Guide to Healing Yourself with Probiotic Foods,
by Donna Schwenk

GORGEOUS FOR GOOD:
A Simple 30-Day Program for Lasting Beauty—Inside and Out,
by Sophie Uliano

THE EARTH DIET:
Your Complete Guide to Living Using Earth's Natural Ingredients,
by Liana Werner-Gray

All of the above are available at your local bookstore,
or may be ordered by contacting Hay House (see next page).

FREE E-NEWSLETTERS FROM HAY HOUSE, THE ULTIMATE RESOURCE FOR INSPIRATION

Be the first to know about Hay House's dollar deals, free downloads, special offers, affirmation cards, giveaways, contests, and more!

 Get exclusive excerpts from our latest releases and videos from *Hay House Present Moments*.

 Enjoy uplifting personal stories, how-to articles, and healing advice, along with videos and empowering quotes, within *Heal Your Life*.

 Have an inspirational story to tell and a passion for writing? Sharpen your writing skills with insider tips from *Your Writing Life*.

Sign Up Now!

Get inspired, educate yourself, get a complimentary gift, and share the wisdom!

http://www.hayhouse.com/newsletters.php

Visit www.hayhouse.com to sign up today!

  HealYourLife.com

LOVE & PEACE